MARCELO BIELSA'S BRILLIANT LEEDS LADS

The Men Who Lit Up The Premiership

Graham Gordon

LIST OF CONTENTS

PART ONE

*THE MAESTRO: MARCELO BIELSA'S
SEVEN GREATEST GAMES*

CHAPTER 1

MAKING LIVERPOOL SWEAT BLOOD

At 5:25 pm on Saturday, September 12 2020 Marcelo Bielsa stepped onto the Anfield turf for Leeds' first Premiership match in sixteen years. The Premier League computer had thrown up the most demanding game imaginable–away to the eighteen point margin reigning Champions, the club who'd won the Champions League the season before that.

Liverpool's path to global supremacy had begun in 1959 with the appointment of Bill Shankly as manager. Extrovert and voluble, Shankly was a man of a very different stripe to Marcelo Bielsa. He also held strong socialist views much like those of Howard Wilkinson. He would certainly have approved of Marcelo Bielsa – scion of a renowned Argentinian Justicialist family –instructing the Leeds players in his first season with them to spend an hour picking up litter so as to remind them of their privileged position vis-à-vis the fans. That in itself echoed Wilkinson's decision to take his Leeds squad underground to a mineshaft so they got to know how hard coal miners had to work-something which would have been applauded by Shankly had he lived to hear of it.

As soon as Bielsa emerged from the tunnel, Liverpool manager Juergen Klopp strode over to greet him. Twelve years younger and three inches taller, Klopp had his big red and white hat pulled down to his eyebrows and was all smiles above his greying beard. Flashing his gleaming Garston teeth, Klopp clapped his left arm round Bielsa's shoulder and seized the Argentinian's hand in a vice-like grip. In the pre-match buildup, he'd already warned Leeds that they'd face "a baptism of fire." When Bielsa spoke a few words in English, Klopp nodded in exaggerated surprise. As he extricated himself from Klopp's Trumpian handshake, Bielsa's half smile vanished and he set his face like flint as he proceeded to the bright red visitors' bench and seated himself in front of it on his blue mobile bucket seat.

At various times during all games Bielsa alternates between pacing briskly in the technical zone, sitting on his mobile seat and crouching by the touchline. It's his way of dealing with the back pain that's troubled him since his playing career was cut short.

Staring down lost in thought, Marcelo realised the cameras were on him and looked up inscrutably. Handsome in his youth, robustly dignified now in his sixth decade, he listened respectfully as the PA system boomed out the Anfield anthem, 'You'll Never Walk Alone.'

In the stands, Andrea Radrizzani, the man who'd had the wisdom to bring Bielsa to Elland Road, braved the chilly Merseyside murk undaunted. Yet John W Henry, Liverpool's multibillionaire American owner and his glamorous wife, the former Linda Pizzuti, were nowhere to be seen. They may well have been relaxing aboard Henry's $68 million superyacht, the 'Elysian', thousands of miles away in the Florida sunshine.

Radrizzani, Milanese by birth, Leeds' owner for three years, celebrated his forty-sixth birthday two days before with his elegant ex-model wife Nedine Vos, a South African. So it's no surprise that he's fluent in English. He looks at least ten years younger than his actual age and his youthful attitude's key to his commitment to the club. When Bielsa narrowly failed to get promotion to the

Premiership in his first season, sceptics were quick to suggest that Radrizzani was about to sell Leeds. He did no such thing, affirming that he had a long-term vision for the Whites. "I am like a child" he said- "I want to make my dream come true."

Ironically it had been Liverpool's most famous player, Sir Kenny Dalglish, who'd first fired the Italian's dream. At a VIP football dinner four years previously, Radrizzani found himself seated next to Dalglish. Disclosing his ambition to own an English club but admitting he had no idea which one he should go for, he was impressed with Dalglish's suggestion that he should invest in Leeds United. "They're the sleeping giants of the game", the Scotsman added. Radrizzani took his advice and never looked back.

Earlier, Sky presenter, the astute and articulate Kelly Cates, daughter of Sir Kenny Dalglish, had announced "and now we're going over to hear the thoughts of Marcelo Bielsa." Yet that was precisely what the huge viewing audience didn't truly hear. Bielsa spoke as always through an interpreter and, for the 2020-1 season, he had a new one. Andres Clavijo was a Colombian in his early thirties, a graduate in sports science, a former video analyst for Queens Park Rangers, who'd been living in London for eleven years and spoke with an Estuary accent. Unfortunately Clavijo was palpably nervous and seemed to struggle rendering Bielsa's cultured Spanish into vibrant English. Already, in the pre-match press conference Marcelo had to tell him to speak more loudly and had corrected a mistranslation. It was the first of several awkward moments between head coach and interpreter which would recur from time to time as the season progressed.

Had lockdown restrictions not been rigorously enforced, the clash between Liverpool and Leeds would of course have been a sell-out with Yorkshire fans penned into one half of the Lower Anfield stand and competing with Scousers, Scandies and the rest of them for vocal supremacy. In the absence of the supporters, it was Sky who would occupy the limelight. Here Leeds' former star striker turned pundit, Jimmy Hasselbaink, found himself outnumbered by fellow pundit and ex-Liverpool midfield enforcer Graeme Souness plus, on commentary, Liverpool's recently retired centre back, Jamie Carragher, who shared the mic with the septuagenarian Cestrian Martin Tyler.

Liverpool were in robust red, shirts sponsored by long established multi-national bankers, Standard Chartered. Leeds were in immaculate white with front-of-shirt branding by sports betting company, SBOTOP.

The scene is set, let battle begin!

Liverpool kick off and pump an aerial ball forward. It's decisively headed away by Leeds' right back, Luke Ayling. Ayling's a key figure, acting skipper, playing alongside a vulnerable central defence in the absence of rugged captain Liam Cooper, injured on Scotland duty. Bielsa's been obliged to field a makeshift pairing, the inexperienced Dutchman Pascal Struijk and the recently recruited Robin Koch, a German international. But Ayling can play in central defence if need be. He can be relied on to give all for the cause. He was the one who greeted Marcelo Bielsa's arrival at Elland Road in 2018 with the words "he's the greatest coach in the world so we'll do everything he says, yeah!"

Scarcely a minute gone and Liverpool mount a dangerous attack. Nabi Keita, their Guinean midfielder, signed from Leipzig two years ago but has never quite fulfilled expectations at Anfield; the Reds' bench urge him on to try his luck against the Premiership newcomers. He neatly passes beyond Struijk to play Roberto Firmino clean through. Fortunately the stellar Brazilian hesitates and Leeds' young French keeper, Illan Meslier, only twenty years of age, half clears the ball with his feet before it's booted out of danger by the bearded Pole, Mateusz Klich.

Klich's Bielsa most trusted player, virtually undroppable. Fluent in English, Klich fulfils one of Bielsa's key requirements of a footballer, the intelligence to grasp video analysis in detail and to learn from it. Twenty years ahead of his time at the millennium, the Argentinian maestro, who once considered a career in film direction, was already emphasising the critical importance of football videography.

In the second minute young Meslier passes out dangerously wide of Luke Ayling. Ayling stops the ball going over the touchline and is at once challenged by Sadio Mane, Liverpool's Senegalese hotshot. Mane scores every other game for the Reds and has been ranked behind only Messi and Ronaldo in competition for the Ballon d'Or. But now it's Luke Ayling, rejected as a youth by Arsenal, he's had to battle his way up the lower divisions yet he nonchalantly nutmegs Mane.

This is what Marcelo Bielsa has given the Leeds players, unshakeable confidence stemming from his personal charisma and his intense will to win.

Sadly it takes only to the third minute for Liverpool to go ahead. But that's thanks to a harsh penalty given by referee Michael Oliver. Mo Salah, the Kop's 'Egyptian King', shoots, the ball strikes Koch on the knee and bounces up to his right hand. Luke Ayling leads the protest, when Mr Oliver gives him his cold eyed Geordie hard man stare – as if to say 'listen, I've been reffing since I was 14, I know what it's all about!' Ayling returns the stare with interest. "The ball popped up off his knee!" he asserts. Koch doesn't plead his own case, he looks meekly resigned. Bielsa never protests referees' decisions, it's pointless anyway but he leaves it to his captain to establish a positive mindset for the ref's future judgments.

Meanwhile Salah, hair and beard freshly trimmed, fills his lungs with air before he lashes the ball through Meslier as if he isn't even there.

Ostentatiously applauded by Juergen Klopp who seems to think everything's unfolding as he knew it would all along, Liverpool mount a succession of quick, slick, accurate passes. Until the eighth minute Leeds remained pinned in their own half.

Then wily Spanish veteran Pablo Hernandez, who created more than three hundred chances during the Whites' days in the Championship, curls a clever chip which Liverpool centre back Joe Gomez can only head weakly out. Klich heads it down, Jack Harrison neatly evades Alexander-Arnold, the Scouse right back, overrated as far as defending's concerned. Harrison jabs a pass to the dreadlocked Portuguese winger Helder Costa. Costa actually puts the ball in the net but he's flagged offside, a correct decision this time.

Leeds, encouraged by their fine move, visibly become bolder with Klich and Hernandez, each of them strong and clever, combining well in midfield. And it's really striking how Patrick Bamford, the man the pundits said would never cut it in the Premiership, is baffling the Reds' central defence with his intelligent, evasive movements. Come to think of it, when you consider that the Dutchman Virgil van Dijk's universally acknowledged as the best centre back in the world, that's really something for a centre forward to be proud of.

11 minutes and 11 seconds, the Whites equalise with an absolutely superb goal. It begins with Kalvin Phillips, standing alone deep in his own half. He gestures to Meslier for the ball, when he gets it, he looks up and sees that Arnold's slack marking, not within ten yards of Jack Harrison, who's on the touchline. Phillips skips for a moment then launches a wonderful 30 yard aerial ball straight to Harrison.

Arnold belatedly reacts but Harrison marvellously traps the ball at full stretch on the toe of his left boot and in the blink of an eye he flicks it beyond Arnold then, lengthening his stride, he surges beyond the flummoxed full-back and closes to the edge of the box. Gomez and Arnold desperately try to stop him, Arnold vainly tries to seize his shorts but Jack Harrison shrugs the pair of them off and cracks a first-time shot low beyond Alisson Becker-the keeper disconcerted by the speed and panache of it all.

The South Americans on the Peacock bench, all a generation younger than Marcelo, spring up in jubilation, the first to react is Pablo Quiroga, Bielsa's right-hand man; he's been with him for many years now, a former PE teacher and an expert in physical conditioning, he punches the air with both hands. Even more emphatic is the Chilean video analysis expert Diego Reyes. Then there's Diego Flores, another Argentinian, he has a really good command of English, acquired while he was studying in Ireland; if Leeds have lost, and Bielsa goes into the dressing room to summarise the reasons why, he speaks in Spanish leaving Flores to translate-or Marcos Abad, the Spanish goalkeeping coach, formerly Bielsa's interpreter.

For all his intellect, Marcelo Bielsa's not a natural linguist and he finds English more difficult than the French which he spoke when he was with Marseille and Lille, just too many clustered consonants for a speaker of Romance languages. Bielsa will be criticised by unthinking persons for not speaking in English at press conferences but his attitude's one of respect not contempt, he wishes to explain himself to the maximum and can only do that via an interpreter. That said, his grasp of basic English is more than sufficient to communicate with his players and Kalvin Phillips has assessed it as "surprisingly good."

Even Marcelo himself's taken back by the speed of this goal, he's calmly sipping a cup of coffee one moment then he punches the air with his left fist the next, shouting "yes!!" It's not only the fact of the equaliser but the way in which it was conceived and executed by two players he personally transformed –Phillips' displaying vision and geometrical precision, Harrison revealing tremendous skill and ruthless despatch.

Three years earlier while analysing video footage of Phillips, Bielsa came to three specific conclusions about the 22-year-old. He could "transfer the ball to a better space than the one in which he found it, cover for the defenders when the full backs went into all-out attack and, if the side came under attack, he would position himself to repel it."

Bielsa then moved Kalvin Phillips back into a role as a defensive midfielder capable of instigating attacks from a deep lying position. He became the linchpin of Bielsa's Leeds, a key cog in the machine which would eventually secure the club's long desired return to the Premiership.

As for Jack Harrison, his arrival at Elland Road on loan from Manchester City coincided with Marcelo Bielsa taking over the reins. Bielsa knew City weren't noted for patience in nurturing English talent and he was also aware that, while with their sister club New York City, Harrison had been studying for a degree at Wake Forrest University. Harrison soon realised that, in Bielsa, he had a coach who was, to all intents and purposes, an unrivalled professor of football. Bielsa, for his part, quickly noted a young man not only highly skilful but a dedicated student eager to learn.

Leeds' players don't indulge in any narcissistic celebrations; indeed, regardless of Phillips' and Harrison's trendy topknots – same as Luke Ayling –they're distinctly old school as they shake hands and clap each other on the back. Bielsa detests any undue celebration regarding it as potentially undermining concentration.

With Juergen Klopp plainly shaken and gesticulating impatiently to his players, the Reds are almost reprieved by a blunder from Meslier who's out of his area when he passes the ball to Mane of all people and promptly finds it lobbed back over his head, fortunately Robertson's offside at the time.

Leeds are only able to maintain parity for ten minutes before they succumb at a corner, van Dijk hits an excellent long ball from the D finding marauding Scottish full-back Andy Robertson, Robertson tries to hook it over Hernandez' head but Pablo gets his napper to it though he's obliged to concede the flag kick; actually he disputes it, claiming Robertson shoved him over the dead ball line, but he doesn't persist.

When Robertson takes the corner there's a goalmouth scramble-Kalvin Phillips, a tough lad from the rough streets of Armley, barges rugged Geordie Jordan Henderson out of the way yet Koch loses van Dijk; the German rookie fails to bulldoze his way past slimjim Sadio Mane as he should have done and he's nowhere near the big Dutchman as he leaps into the air and powerfully heads the ball down through Meslier's gloves.

Questions have to be asked about the suitability of Robin Koch for the hurly-burly of the Premiership, Liam Cooper would have been in his element there and Struijk's a hefty lad no worries. Presently Bielsa's looking to capture the Spanish international Diego Llorente and Victor Orta's working on the deal.

The thing is that the Spaniard Orta, Leeds' Director of Football, a crucial figure in bringing Bielsa to the club, has been stymied in negotiations for Ben White, Brighton's splendid young centre back who'd been on loan at Elland Road for a year and had endeared himself to the fans. But it didn't matter what money Brighton were offered for his permanent signature–18 million, 20 million, 25 million, even thirty-they turned it all down and it was rumoured they were hanging back in the belief that Liverpool would be tempted to come in for him; that didn't materialize!

The central defensive problem is what'll dog Leeds' early-season, Victor Orta got fed up with inflated English prices and looking abroad, he recruited Koch on the cheap from Freiburg in the Bundesliga; in monetary terms a bargain at £13 million but had he been fobbed off with a fellow who just couldn't cut the mustard in the rough-and-tumble of the Premiership? Time would tell.

Meanwhile Leeds move forward, Bielsa has instilled the belief that, regardless of a negative scoreline, you press on undaunted. Ayling, continuing in fine form, evades Henderson, he's just as powerful as his opposite number the Reds' permanent captain, he strokes a brilliant pass beyond Gomez and finds Patrick Bamford in the D. Brazilian goalkeeper Alisson Becker, universally acclaimed as the best in the world, shows Bamford to one side where Robertson's tracking back. Bamford, unflustered, coolly turns the ball back to Klich who crosses for Harrison, Arnold's belatedly learned his lesson and is keeping tabs on the winger, nowt doin' there.

Phillips serves up another fine crossfield ball for Harrison who traps it with ease; looks like the start of another dangerous move but the whistle goes for offside, the culprit's Costa. Bielsa's furious, finger pointed to his head, he shouts "use the brain! didn't you SEE that?"

Rather than an equalizer, Leeds almost concede another goal when Struijk, hitherto faultless, unaccountably flings out a boot at a cross almost as if he were intent on lobbing his own keeper. Mercifully Meslier leaps up, all two metres of him and pushes the ball over the bar for a corner from which nothing comes; here's a strange thing, it requires a desperate save from your own teammate to give a keeper the confidence he wasn't showing before.

Nothing boosts any team more than fine goalkeeping and, in the 29th minute, the Whites equalize again, Meslier kicks long to Stuart Dallas. Dallas is playing left back today but he's known for his versatility in several positions. Another thing about him is this, that he's probably the fittest man in the entire Leeds squad, he flourished in the so-called 'murder ball' sessions which Bielsa introduced. Marcelo Bielsa's other great innovation in the evolution of football coaching was his insistence on superlative fitness. He'd shocked Argentina by dispensing with the old style foot-on-the ball enganche, the likes of Juan Roman Riquelme. Languid buildup was out and fast-paced inter-passing was in.

So far in the match Dallas has run hither and thither ensuring that Mo Salah couldn't find space. Scarcely out of breath, the Ulsterman now brings off a brilliant pass from his thigh, bypassing Keita and finding Klich. The Pole instantly flicks a return beyond the advancing Gomez and back to Dallas. Dallas, on the halfway line, looks ahead, seeking to breach the Liverpool back line fast. He aims a long ball for Bamford; it looks as if it'll be comfortably dealt with by van Dijk standing in the D but the big Dutchman elects to stick out a nonchalant leg– and fails to trap the ball. Alisson closes in desperately–this is Patrick Bamford's critical moment, faced with the world's best keeper, will he fluff it? Not a bit of it, he keeps his cool even as van Dijk lunges in, desperate to atone for his error. Alisson slides towards him with his right leg extended but Bamford gets there first and clips the ball clean away to find the net on the second bounce. Yes, Patrick Bamford, the man the pundits derided as not good enough, has become a dangerous Premiership striker.

Patrick Bamford was Bielsa's first signing, brought to the club within weeks of the Argentinian's arrival at Elland Road. Rapidly assessing video footage of centre forwards from Championship clubs, Bielsa picked out Middlesborough's Bamford on the basis of his intelligent movement, rarely straying offside and often confounding defences with his evasive switch of position.

Sadly Leeds concede again even more quickly than the first time around, Sadio Mane's off on a potentially dangerous burst, he just manages to get past Ayling's tackle and he's staggering from his momentum when Hernandez fouls him as he falls. It's a gratuitous blunder seeing the Senegalese star's nowhere near goal at the time. Marcelo Bielsa's exasperated- "aargh Pablo!!" he cries as he rolls his eyes upward in despair at the Spaniard's folly.

Liverpool exact retribution from the free kick, taken by Henderson. Struijk succeeds in rebuffing it but, instead of heading the ball back in the direction it came from, he plants it at the feet of the unmarked Mo Salah, Salah responds with an instant right foot trap followed by a fearsomely fast left foot half volley which flies into the roof of the net just inside the junction of post and crossbar. The often overused phrase "unstoppable shot" is totally accurate in this case. So's another phrase from the football lexicon-"world-class" yet Salah's a truly great player, against anyone else Struijk might have got away with his error.

Now disagreement breaks out in the Whites' ranks; Struijk gives Dallas a reproachful look, Dallas has so far been tracking Salah all the way but this time he didn't. Stuart's not an aggressive guy but he frowns and taps his chest saying "that's not my fault, y' know." What Struijk, still a comparative novice, has yet to realise is that Bielsa doesn't insist on strict man-to-man marking at a set piece, preferring to rely on players to assume personal responsibility. Bielsa discourages argument between players and now he turns away to calmly check his stopwatch –still only 33 minutes gone.

After an inevitable lull in this titanic clash-one which lasts some six minutes-Liverpool have a quick break, Henderson –Salah – Mane, he shoots from an angle and Meslier saves well with his legs just as the whistle blows for offside.

Besides his role in creating a goal for Jack Harrison, Kalvin Phillips has been very effective in defensive midfield, neutralising Liverpool's deep lying centre forward Firmino.

Just before half-time there's an excellent move from Leeds which breaks down with Costa. It involves Ayling, Phillips and Klich before Costa claims a penalty from a minimal touch by the backtracking Salah, Mr Oliver brushes it aside, quite rightly so. Costa's on dangerous ground here. As he demonstrated in the notorious match with Aston Villa in 2019-when he ordered Leeds to deliberately concede a goal after they'd scored themselves when Villa had a man down injured-Bielsa will have no truck with the slightest hint of cheating.

Whereas on Leeds' left flank, Harrison has worked hard to check the forward runs of Alexander-Arnold, normally a big feature of Liverpool's attacking play, Costa's been comparatively indolent on the opposite wing leaving Ayling to contain Robertson's rapid bursts on his own.

At half time media underestimation of Leeds United shows up as soon as the Whites walk off. "There's a gulf between Liverpool and them" insists Jamie Carragher and Martin Tyler nonchalantly agrees. It's a theme which will be taken up time and time again by other pundits, BT as well as Sky. As the season unfolds they will dub Bielsa's Leeds "the great entertainers" pretending that's a compliment when it's nothing of the kind!

For its opening ten minutes, the second half's a dismal anticlimax after the heroics of the first. Liverpool and Leeds cancel each other out and the only thing to note is Illan Meslier confidently calling out his teammates after an underhit pass by Ayling, aimed for Dallas, almost lets Salah in and the young keeper only just gets there in time to kick the ball clear. He gives off to Dallas first then he doesn't hesitate to take his skipper to task.

Marcelo Bielsa's pacing his technical zone deep in thought – how to get Leeds going again? Normally he's not a man for the long ball aimed over the top but he'd already instructed Robin Koch to try that as a surprise move if all else fails. Koch has noted Arnold's lapses of concentration and now he pumps a high one for Harrison-who lobs the keeper; reacting belatedly, Arnold chases after the high bouncing ball, trying to head it for a corner, he only succeeds in dumping it into his own net. Jack's jubilation's cut short, he's given offside, a replay shows it's clearly the correct decision.

Juergen Klopp has also been mulling over the Reds' failure to pick up things where they left off from the first session. Just before the hour, he withdraws the utterly ineffective Keita and brings on the shaven-headed Brazilian midfielder, Fabinho. Brainy and brawny, Fabinho would surely have been selected in the first case only for his manager's concern that he'd be jetlagged after a long trip from an international game in Brazil.

Fabinho immediately gives new life to the Reds, he beats Phillips to the ball and lays it off swift and long to Mo Salah on the halfway line, well beyond Dallas; Salah's beautiful pass, straight as an arrow to the feet of Mane; with the two Leeds' centre backs on either side of him, Mane lets the ball run, he's confident that he'll outpace them and score.

Here's a very encouraging sign of hope for Leeds United, Robin Koch sticks to his guns, he challenges Mane shoulder to shoulder and outmuscles him, nullifying the manifest danger.

This was an electrifying Liverpool move and now Leeds respond with one of their own, Pascal Struijk uncorks a colossal long ball, it rolls to a halt by the corner flag, Jack Harrison gets on it; calmly back to Dallas, then a brilliant high-speed bout of triangular passing between Dallas and Hernandez; Dallas looks to steers the ball across the six yard box where Bamford's gaining on Gomez. But Alisson parries to Fabinho who confidently clears.

A real jolt for Leeds, Fabinho executes far more than just a clearance, he finds his compatriot Firmino with a tremendous long pass, Firmino gets past Phillips in the blink of an eye, his forward pass finds Mane, Mane and Salah swap passes at high speed, Mane surges on, it only remains for him to find the net but, to Leeds' immense relief, he wallops the ball high over the bar.

Apart from the finish this was Liverpool at their devastating best in the kind of form which swept aside the best opposition in the Premiership and in the Champions League. It's no disgrace to Leeds that they couldn't withstand it, indeed it was their own exhilarating attack that provoked the Reds' sensational counter.

Suddenly the match has been re-energised at an even higher level than in the first half.

At this point Marcelo Bielsa makes a double substitution; first he withdraws Pablo Hernandez. Hernandez has done a lot of good work but, at 35 years of age, it would be a tall order to ask him to compete with speed the likes of which he's never encountered before.

On comes Rodrigo, the Brazilian-born Spanish international, Leeds' record purchase at £27 million, highly skilful and intelligent, yes and also six years younger than Hernandez.

Bielsa's second change is more questionable. True, Bamford's form in the second half has been below what he achieved in the first session yet to replace him with the Welsh lad Tyler Roberts is a surprising decision.

Three minutes later Klopp withdraws his skipper, Henderson who, recovering from an injury, is beginning to fade. On comes the teenage Scouser Curtis Jones, a skilful attacking midfielder and mature enough to have already captained Liverpool in an FA Cup match.

Then, in the 66th minute, it's 3-3. Leeds bring off a tremendous equaliser executed with intelligence and panache. Stuart Dallas intercepts a careless throw in by Arnold and heads the ball forward to Phillips, Curtis Jones is said to be streetwise but he's no match for Kalvin Phillips; having kept Jones at bay, Phillips looks for an opening yet Rodrigo, dashing back, has already spotted that, far away on the right flank, Robertson's slack marking Helder Costa. How to get the ball out there? Rodrigo takes over from Phillips and glides a pass back to Klich, Klich's right on his wavelength, he makes sure to find Costa and anticipates a return pass, Costa's too quick for Robertson and he steers the ball beyond the bemused van Dijk bouncing into Mateusz Klich's path. In a flash Klich traps the ball, coolly waits for it to drop then wheels and blasts home a half volley so fierce that in empty Anfield the sound of it striking the base of the far stanchion resonates like a rifle shot. Big Matt, the bearded Pole, grits his teeth then clenches his fist, this is the best goal he's ever scored.

As a beaming Rodrigo hugs Klich in delight, Marcelo Bielsa salutes the strike with an upraised left arm, he knew what to expect from Klich. But the head coach wants victory not just a share of the points. "Again! Go again!!" he shouts.

At the edge of his technical zone, Juergen Klopp's yelling his head off. He can't let his Champions be worsted in the first match of the season by these Yorkshire upstarts, is that what he reckons?

Relying on their typical attacking ploys-this time the cross is from Robertson- Liverpool cause problems in the Leeds' box, Salah's on the ball but the way it falls he has to strike it with his right foot not his favoured left and he gasps in annoyance as he thumps it high over the bar.

75 minutes and a mistake by Firmino, his weak pass intended for Arnold's intercepted by Harrison, Firmino chases after Harrison and cynically shoves him even as he trips him, resulting in a yellow card from Mr Oliver.

The freekick, from all of 35 yards, is taken by Kalvin Phillips who scored in similar fashion against Blackburn in the Championship. He leans confidently back, lofts the ball over the leaping wall and curls it round aiming for just inside the near post; Alisson, shocked by the speed of it, hurls himself full length and just fails to get his fingertips to it as it skims the upright. Phillips is left anguished by his proximity to a majestic strike.

Salah's pepped up, he's seen what Leeds can do, he swiftly prompts Wijnaldum who shoots strongly, Klich bravely puts his body on the line, he crashes to the turf as he brings off a tumbling block, Salah gets on the ball and forces a corner, from which van Dijk emerges totally in the clear and brusquely batters the ball home from close range.

But the whistle goes, Mr Oliver's disallowed it and van Dijk's furious, he charges towards the man in black −"hey ref" he snarls and points an accusing finger. In the technical zone Juergen Klopp towers over the fourth official, Mike Dean, and demands redress while van Dijk pursues his tirade− "that was never a foul!" But what Mr Oliver's noticed was that when the big Dutchman broke clear of Koch, the German sprang after him straightaway only to be knocked flat by Curtis Jones.

Less than 10 minutes to go, Bielsa's noted that Klich hasn't really recovered after lying winded from the impact of Wynaldum's point-blank shot; he subs him, Klich's unhappy about that but on comes Jamie Shackleton, 20 years of age and only 5'6" tall but he's a tough Leeds lad and a clever one, he was at St Wilfrid's Sixth Form College when he opted for a football career.

Anyone doubting that Marcelo Bielsa can speak basic English should watch him giving detailed instructions to Shackleton, gesticulating as he does so, Shackleton listens earnestly and nods his head.

Tyler Roberts has made very little impact. It would be unfair to call him a passenger because he's tried to the best of his ability without being able to contribute anything significant.

Now Liverpool are besieging the Leeds goal, Meslier's almost caught out by a mishit Arnold cross which drifts just beyond the far post, then Koch get lucky when he stretches out a leg looking to block a shot from Firmino, it could have gone anywhere but it goes for a corner- which Leeds survive.

Next Firmino wastes a good chance after Salah found him with a brilliant turn and pass to confound Dallas, Firmino fluffs his shot, it rebounds off Ayling and when Firmino tries to get back on the ball, Shackleton shows him away at the expense of a corner.

In some ways it seems as if Liverpool are bound to prevail; with only three minutes left on the clock Leeds have held firm so far. Then –catastrophe! From Robertson's corner, Ayling, hounded by van Dijk, tries to clear but the ball loops up high, Rodrigo's backing up in defence, he outjumps Gomez to win a defensive header but it falls straight to Fabinho- Rodrigo's shockingly clumsy challenge, dangling a nonchalant leg, over which Fabinho obligingly falls, every single Leeds man stands hands clasped to his head in dismay, Rodrigo looks mortified, he momentarily closes his eyes, opening them only to stare down at the Anfield turf as if he wished it'd swallow him. Mr Oliver points to the spot, one of the easiest decisions he's ever had to make.

Salah steps up, does his deep breathing act and effortlessly dispatches the spot kick. Marcelo Bielsa squats in the technical zone, his head's down, he seems momentarily disconsolate. Then he springs up again shouting "come on! come on!!" Leeds have equalised three times and there's just a chance they could do it again, four minutes indicated for stoppage time.

Phillips responds to the call, he hits a fine dropping cross right into the heart of the Liverpool goalmouth, Koch jumps up trying to get a header on it, sadly Harrison, overeager, goes for the same ball, Gomez heads it away but it loops up and only finds Ayling, Bielsa's in full cry –"win this!"- and Pablo Quiroga shouts the same, Shackleton brushes aside Wijnaldum, Liverpool's Dutch midfielder-who's underperformed for much of the game, the ball breaks to Roberts, looking to put it back in the mixer, he overhits his cross.

The final whistle sounds, Bielsa acknowledges Klopp with a fist push but breaks free of the Liverpool bosses' hug. Klopp turns to the cameras, his exclamation "wow!!!" says it all, this was a relief not a triumph. Liverpool have three points but Leeds made them sweat blood to get them.

Postscript

Marcelo Bielsa's main task after the narrow defeat at Anfield was the restoration of team morale and, in particular, that of Rodrigo who blamed himself for conceding the late penalty which, in the postmatch press conference, Bielsa dismissed as "a contingency of the game during the last ten minutes when Liverpool got on top and already had several good chances to score."

Bielsa was very well equipped for the task in hand. He was known to devour books on psychology and regularly emailed his players with advice gleaned from articles on psychological matters.

In one way it helped that the next match, at Elland Road, was against fellow promotees Fulham who'd finished the Championship 12 points behind Leeds. By now Cooper had returned, and Helder Costa quickly opened the scoring. Costa notched another goal, Klich converted a penalty and Bamford scored once again. Yet from being 4-1 ahead Leeds complacently allowed Fulham to get two goals back. Bielsa needed all his powers of exhortation to ensure that the Londoners, a mediocre side by Premiership standards, didn't snatch a draw. The game finished 4-3 to the Whites.

The next match was at Bramall Lane- a Yorkshire derby. At that early stage of the season it wasn't yet clear that Sheffield United would be relegation candidates. They played with their customary vigour and it took a convincing late header from Patrick Bamford to seal three points with a one nil win. Meslier distinguished himself with two phenomenal saves. Roberts was keeping Rodrigo out of the starting lineup yet, for all his efforts, Roberts' end product was meagre.

It would take another outstanding performance against a top-class Premiership team –and the avoidance of defeat-to convince the lads that they could cut the mustard at the highest level. No better opportunity could have presented itself than the arrival of Manchester City, Champions with a record points tally in 2018-19, to put the unhappy memory of Anfield behind them three weeks to the day later.

CHAPTER 2

MIXING IT WITH MIGHTY MAN CITY

In their colossal buildup to a match scheduled for October 3, Sky sought to define it in terms of a contrast in both achievement and record between the two managers, Pep Guardiola and Marcelo Bielsa. Guardiola's been fawned on for years by the English media who've emphasised his successes both domestically with Barcelona, Bayern Munich and Manchester City and in the Champions League with the Catalan club.

As for Bielsa, there was a pundit tendency to parrot his undeserved nickname of 'El Loco' and to claim that "he's never actually won anything." As far as two Clausuras and Argentina's victory in the Olympic Games was concerned, either they were unaware of them or dismissed them as being of scant consequence. The brevity of Bielsa's sojourns at Lazio and Lille were stressed but without the context of his perfectly reasonable objections to the methods of player recruitment at those clubs.

Pep Guardiola, on the other hand, spoke of Marcelo Bielsa with the utmost respect. It was Bielsa, after all, whom he'd sought out for advice at the start of his own managerial career. He's on record as saying that the Argentinian's "the most authentic coach in football history." Regarding the upcoming encounter between City and Leeds, Guardiola reminded the media that, on the three previous occasions when he was with Barcelona and Bielsa was at Athletic Bilbao, he'd twice had to pull all the stops out to win against a club with far fewer resources than the Catalan giants. On the third occasion Bilbao had held Barcelona to a draw. "It's always been difficult against Marcelo's teams and I'm sure it'll be just the same against Leeds" he conceded.

In his own pre-match interview, when asked about "ideas which Pep has taken from you", Marcelo Bielsa replied obliquely that "I don't consider that he's taken any ideas from me." The next question concerned City's shocking defeat at home the previous week when Leicester City trounced them 5-2 and Jamie Vardy scored a hat-trick. "It could be said this is a good time to play Manchester City" claimed a Sky interviewer. Bielsa brusquely dismissed this silly notion countering "I have the feeling that they will gain strength in adversity." As in previous interviews and press conferences in England, Leeds' head coach, whilst scrupulously polite, demonstrated a mentality far in advance of his interlocutors.

It had been pouring down with rain for ages before kick-off and the slick surface of the pitch seemed ideal for Guardiola's brand of possession-based football. His style was one which sought to remove the element of risk and was in total contrast to Bielsa's adventurous approach.

City were undeniably disadvantaged by the absence through injury of their great Argentinian centre forward Sergio Aguero and, to a lesser extent, that of Brazilian striker Gabriel Jesus. But the Manchester club's bigger problem was their failure, despite massive investment, to recruit defenders anywhere near the standard of their gifted midfielders and attackers. Their oil-rich Abu Dhabi owners scarcely question Guardiola's demands for new players and they'd just shelled out no less than 61 million quid for the Portuguese centre back Ramon Dias, bought from Benfica. With his gifted compatriot Bernardo Silva stood down as well as Brazilian captain Fernandinho and John Stones, Guardiola selected Frenchman Aymeric Laporte, who'd spoken of how much Bielsa had helped him when they were both with Athletic Bilbao.

Leeds were not at full strength. Jack Harrison was ineligible to play against his parent club. Eager to be present at the encounter, he sat behind the subs' quarters, a lonely figure, cap pulled down to his eyebrows and enveloped in a cloak-like white overcoat.

Before kick-off Bielsa walked briskly to the City bench, shook hands with Guardiola and exchanged a few words before Leeds in pristine white readied themselves to face the Manchester club in their surprisingly grim all-black kit.

Leeds' moment of maximum danger comes, just as it had against Liverpool, in the third minute. This time they survive. Luke Ayling's foul on Raheem Sterling's all of 30 yards out and wide left but it's well within range for Kevin de Bruyne.

In the absence of Aguero and following the return of veteran David Silva to Spain, Kevin de Bruyne's undoubtedly City's most dangerous player. At 29 years of age, the still boyish-looking Belgian is truly world-class, known for sublime technical skill, an acute football brain and a fearsome shot. Now he strikes a ferocious free kick, accelerating, curling and dipping. It crashes against the near post with a helluva thwack before Leeds desperately clear the rebound in a goalmouth scramble.

Sky commentator Martin Tyler blames Illan Meslier for adjusting his weight late, alleging his so-called naïveté. In actual fact de Bruyne's fulminating delivery had the potential to embarrass any keeper. Yet the Belgian looks glumly disappointed with his failure to score, his ginger locks plastered to his napper in the pissing rain.

Temporarily stunned by their narrow survival, Leeds remain penned in their own half for fully seven minutes as City strive to turn possession superiority into goals. Guardiola prowls his techni-cal zone, baldheaded and grey bearded, bellowing his troops on. Nearby Bielsa squats, his saturated glasses removed in the continu-ing downpour. "Come on, boys!" he shouts –"Leeds, come on!!"

City are in their element on the rain-slicked surface. De Bruyne runs midfield like a rock band frontman high on amphetamine. Ahead of him are two dangerous attackers, the heavily hyped Englishman Sterling and the still somewhat underrated Algerian, Riyad Mahrez. Mahrez, skinny and suavely bearded, honed his skills and sharpened his soccer brain as a boy in the strife-strewn streets of Sarcelles. In the opening 15 minutes the possession sta-tistics are truly alarming – 28% to 72%!

The danger mounts by the minute, Meslier's inaccurate goal kick leaves Phillips with too much to do, de Bruyne sweeps the ball past him in a second; the Belgian dashes 20 yards at top speed then shoots, Robin Koch brings off a bloody good block, the German looks far more at ease against City's precision buildup-almost Bundesliga style-than he did against Liverpool's heavy metal assault.

It's a corner from which the new boy Dias has a good chance to score, thankfully he puts his header a couple of yards wide.

Bamford, looking desperate to get the Whites going, catches Laporte with a hand across his jaw, the Frenchman makes a meal of it and referee Mike Dean, the diminutive whistler from the Wirral, promptly books Leeds' centre forward.

Alioski's dyed his bonce peroxide blond and this only empha-sizes his bad mistake when he crassly heads Stuart Dallas' header straight back towards him. Obviously Dallas wasn't expecting that, he's wrongfooted and the pallid, low-browed Stockport lad, Phil Foden, nips ahead and shoots, fortunately Liam Cooper gets a block in.

In the 13th minute Leeds finally manage a move, what's more, they might have scored, after endless City inter-passing, Laporte

finally gives the ball away, to Alioski, Leeds move on fast, Alioski –
Dallas –Roberts, Roberts with a really good crossfield ball to Costa,
Costa's short pass back to Ayling, Ayling crosses to the far post and
Alioski outjumps Kyle Walker but heads the ball well wide.

Walker's noted for running forward fast and strong but defensively he's not sound, his reading of the game leaves a lot to be
desired, often he's gormlessly square on and static, that's how little
Alioski got the better of him even though he couldn't make the
most of that.

City resume in their high paced precision passing style, Foden –
Sterling, he beats Ayling with stepovers then cuts the ball back for
Spanish newbie, Ferran Torres; Torres shoots strongly but Dallas
brings off a fine block.

Leeds are stretched to the absolute limit keeping City at bay,
Guardiola's agitated, the men in black must score, he demands. 7-1
advantage in goal attempts is obviously not enough.

Finally, 0-1, City take the lead, a long kick from Meslier seized
on by burly French left back Mendy, he's too strong for Costa, he
barrels forward but even though he makes a bollocks of his forward pass, Liam Cooper gives the ball away to Mahrez, Mahrez'
instant pass wide to Sterling with Ayling not having closed in on
the England international, Sterling embarks on a lateral run,
Cooper, suddenly shaky, fails to get in a tackle; Sterling's looking
to pick his moment and he does so with a curling shot beyond
Phillips and Dallas, craftily placed low into the far corner. "Yes!"
Sterling screams, thumping his chest, determined to convince the
pundits that his days as a duff finisher are well and truly over.

On Sky Gary Neville laconically observes "the only surprise is it
took 17 minutes for City to score."

Three minutes later it looks like they might do so again, Mahrez,
technically excellent and always quickwitted, sends Sterling clear
with a brilliant reverse pass, Sterling tries to be too clever attempting to nutmeg Luke Ayling, he can't do it so Kevin de Bruyne takes

over; he storms goalwards but Mat Klich matches him stride for stride and splendidly blocks the Belgian's shot at the expense of a corner.

If you're measuring supremacy in terms of corners, City have already chalked up five but Leeds not even one. De Bruyne's truly testing corner, Laporte rises above Ayling, fortunately his header's wide.

22 minutes, the onslaught continues, de Bruyne brusquely robs Phillips and plays in Sterling who draws the defence before passing to Foden, Foden's unmarked but he shoots 3 yards wide. It's clear that Guardiola, well aware of Phillips' capacity to instigate attacks from deep midfield, has ordered Mahrez to deny him space.

One glimmer of light in the gloom is that Leeds have shown they can bring off good defensive blocks, on the other hand they've not shown the capacity to constrict City.

It's no disgrace, Mahrez is a very good player and Kevin de Bruyne's a great one.

On the other hand, Leeds have got outstanding collective virtues, tremendous team spirit and superlative fitness. And, though Guardiola had cottoned on to that, his players look like they expected the lads in white to fold. With City miffed that Leeds aren't surrendering, the balance of play begins to change around the 25 minute mark.

Mendy's the one who's most flummoxed by Leeds' revival-he foolishly fouls Costa when two of his teammates were already poised to dispossess the Portuguese winger; Mr Dean books him for his crude blunder. The mountainous left back barges past Helder Costa but ends up perplexed and profusely perspiring as Kalvin Phillips sturdily closes him down. Mendy tries again. But he can only run the ball out over the touchline. Incredibly the lino doesn't spot it and Luke Ayling gets a lecture from Mr Dean for suggesting a visit to Specsavers. Mendy's stressed out with the pace of it all and soon afterwards he's tripping Helder Costa in full flight.

He stands there sweating cobs as the baldheaded Tranmere fan gives him a baleful stare and reaches into a back pocket. He elects to reprieve the big Frenchman and merely brandishes a yellow.

Leeds are coming into it and are gaining a narrow advantage in terms of possession. City look taken aback by the Whites' effrontery, there's almost a lull for a while.

Eight minutes to go before half-time and Leeds start to boss things, Koch begins to move up into midfield, he feeds Dallas, Stuart crosses to Klich, from Klich to Bamford, Bamford gets the better of Dias, he passes to Dallas overlapping at a helluva lick, Dallas surges past Walker even though the stocky Sheffield-born swaggerer looks to have given him a sly nudge, Dallas shoots strongly but Ederson, hitherto almost unemployed, brings off a fine point-blank save at the cost of a corner.

On Sky Gary Neville surmises that Dallas might have won a penalty if he'd gone down as soon as he felt contact from Walker. Neville refrains from any mention of Marcelo Bielsa whose Corinthian standards of fair play Stuart Dallas has impeccably observed.

Leeds' corner results in another one conceded by Laporte; from this City mount a counter-attack in which Mendy's miskick turns into a pass for de Bruyne who surges forward from deep in his own half, Dallas catches up with him and dispossesses him.

Leeds well on top in the approach to half-time, 64% to 36%, Koch moves confidently forward and delivers a bouncing pass for Bamford, Bamford stabs the ball beyond the defender and wide, effectively passing to himself as he drives onto the loose ball taking it right to the byline before cutting it back to Klich on the edge of the area, thence to Costa, he shoots, it goes off Laporte for another corner, but nowt doin.'

One minute into stoppage time and Leeds must surely score, Roberts is fouled, Cooper's very long free kick flummoxes Mendy, he miscontrols and lets Luke Ayling right in, Ayling splendidly sits down Laporte and fires off his shot but it's superbly saved by Ederson with his outstretched right fist. The Brazilian cuts a bizarre figure with his purplish pink jersey below a riot of neck tattoos. Still, he's a tremendous keeper without a doubt.

Marcelo Bielsa makes two big decisions at half-time. It's blatantly obvious that Benjamin Mendy's City's weakest link. Bielsa knows all about big Ben, he had him under his command at Marseille and Mendy was on record praising his Argentinian coach for restoring his self-confidence. The boot's on the other foot now of course and Bielsa reckons he has just the weapon to undermine the big beefy lad from Longjumeau.

Sitting on Leeds' bench there's Ian Poveda Ocampo, a young Londoner of Colombian heritage. Poveda used to be on City's books and must have played many a game in training against Mendy. Poveda's fleet of foot and a useful dribbler prepared to track back, a winger/wingback truth to tell. Bielsa sends him on in place of Alioski who, his one header on goal apart, has contributed nothing.

With Poveda deployed on the right, Costa's switched to the left. He'd struggled physically against Mendy but he has the skill to confound Walker whose defensive weakness has already been in evidence.

The other vital matter is when to introduce Rodrigo. At Bramall Lane the Spaniard had been brought on at half-time. But against City, Bielsa will delay his arrival for a further ten minutes. This might not seem a major difference but in the world of physical fitness it's considerable. Even as the first half concluded, Bielsa was seen conferring in the technical zone with Pablo Quiroga. Pablo is of course an expert on conditioning. They both know that Rodrigo has taken time to adjust to the 'murder ball' sessions which, for the Championship lads, have become a matter of course. So around the 55th minute will be just right to bring on Rodrigo and remove Tyler Roberts, a more than willing worker who's struggling at Premiership level.

Poveda's on, his eyes light up and in next to no time he's roasting the burly Frenchman. Bielsa has also sent Phillips forward to directly instigate attacks. As for Illan Meslier, he's standing soaked to the skin in the relentless rain not having had to make a save against the much-vaunted City attack–a total contrast to his opposite number Ederson.

Leeds cut loose with high-speed interpassing; Dallas to Klich and return and thence to Poveda – on to Ayling but he overhits the cross, very vexed with himself.

Patrick Bamford's not having his best game, epic at Anfield, brilliant at Bramall Lane but just not cutting the mustard here today as he miscontrols in front of goal.

Volubly urged on by Guardiola, City look to respond, Mahrez to Sterling via Foden, Sterling tries a shot but Phillips blocks it and Dallas completes the clearance.

In the 56th minute Rodrigo arrives. Plainly pumped up and looking streamlined from his 'murder ball' sessions, it takes him only two minutes to make a massive difference. Klich prompts him at the earliest opportunity and the stellar Spaniard surges into the box. Laporte confronts him but is shaken off with a sublime soft shoe shuffle before Rodrigo unleashes a thunderbolt only centimetres off target as it slams against the angle of the goal frame leaving the crossbar shuddering from the violent impact. Incredibly Ederson got his fingertips to the ball edging it to safety by the narrowest margin.

From Phillips' corner kick Ederson goes from hero to villain as he paws at a punch. The ball bounces off Mendy and Rodrigo's the first to react, sweeping it in at close range through a tight knot of players.

He celebrates with Brazilian style exuberance. In a matter of moments he's annihilated the memory of his unhappy days at Bolton ten years ago when he was a lad of 19. Andrea Radrizzani and Victor Orta lustily applaud the strike. This is what they paid

Valencia £27 million for, chickenfeed by Manchester City standards of course but a record for Leeds. They resume in their seats peering intently over their black masks while City's elite Emirati owners can only snatch glances on their custom-made $1.6 million 370 inch TV screens in faraway Abu Dhabi.

Poveda continues to torment Mendy yet Guardiola, with goals his priority leaves him in situ and, taking off the ineffective Torres, he introduces the Portuguese, Bernardo Silva, a man of high skill and resolute purpose.

Walker desperately fouls Dallas right on the touchline. Phillips delivers a really good freekick dropping into the goalmouth, Cooper nods it clear of Ederson but only against Rodri's head and thence onto the post. Cooper's flagged offside, a very tight decision.

In the 69th minute the Whites are foiled from seizing the lead due to Ederson's great goalkeeping. Poveda aims a cross for Bamford, the ball ricochets off Laporte but Rodrigo, reacting incredibly fast, leaps up like a salmon, his mighty header from 12 yards looked a certain goal till the Brazilian's phenomenal save diverted it for an uneventful corner.

A minute later the dawdling de Bruyne's ruthlessly robbed by Kalvin Phillips, Kalvin passes promptly to Poveda, Poveda's ball to Rodrigo, he interpasses with the improving Bamford, who beats Rodri and tees up Costa, Costa drives on into the box looking to square the ball to the advancing Dallas but Ramon Dias intercepts. Sliding to the ground same as Costa on the still soaking turf, he's the first to get up and clears the danger. Judged on this incident, City at last look as if they've made an effective albeit expensive acquisition in defence.

Kevin de Bruyne looks proper pissed off, who is this Yorkshire Phillips taking the ball off me with his 'eh up, bud, ya didn't see that comin', did ya?' And up front there's that Rodrigo trying to steal my thunder, I'm the only world class player round here, doesn't he realise?

At 72 minutes Guardiola removes Mendy, not before time, and substitutes the Dutchman Nathan Ake, City only paid Bournemouth 40 million for him!

Finally City hit back, Rodri to Mahrez and the Algerian's incisive instant pass looks as if it'll give the men in black a winner clean against the run of play. Sterling's a greyhound, there's normally no way you can catch him if he has a head start and he eagerly sees himself bagging a brace with only Meslier to beat. Robin Koch seems to be lumbering after him in vain but somehow the lanky German stretches out a leg, adroitly avoids conceding the penalty but dislodges the ball from Sterling's boots with the merest touch of his heel. Lo and behold Sterling's so miffed he merely dribbles it against Meslier as the keeper drops to his knees.

15 minutes to go and Guardiola, who's been furtively sheltering from the pelting rain while Bielsa squats undaunted in the technical zone, emerges with what seems like a safety first move, bringing off the dangerous Mahrez and replacing him with the gritty Brazilian midfield veteran Fernandinho.

Bielsa counters by taking off the tiring Klich and deploying Leeds youngster Leif Davis at left back. But it has to be said, Guardiola's substitution enables City to belatedly regain the bulk of possession with Fernandinho linking up dangerously with Silva.

Then Rodrigo drives upfield and fires a fine pass to free Costa, Costa unwisely ignores the overlapping Dallas, opting instead to give the ball to Davis, it's deflected for a corner, nowt doin.'

Ayling finds Rodrigo, Rodrigo tricks his near namesake Rodri, they've got the same name on the back of their shirts but there the resemblance ends, Leeds' new star passes to the feet of Bamford, Bamford gets a shot in but doesn't trouble Ederson.

Leeds are hard pressed to keep City out in the last ten minutes, the same as they were against Liverpool but there'll be no easy reprieve this time. It seems like Sterling can't accept this, "hey ref, what about that?" he yells as Liam Cooper slides over in defence with his lower arm touching the ball as he lands. Mr Dean's having none of it, quite rightly so and he waves play on. Sterling tries his luck again, bawling his head off that Davis has tripped him, Mr Dean once again correctly ignores his outburst.

In the three minutes of stoppage time Mr Dean does produce a yellow card, it's against Dallas who raked his bootstuds down the back of Silva's heel, a less than saintly end to the Ulsterman's otherwise tremendous display. On Sky Gary Neville insists that Dallas should have been dismissed.

The match ends all square, only two goals to show but nevertheless an exciting and wonderfully fluctuating clash where Leeds have more than held their own against the ex-Champions

At the close Marcelo Bielsa's smiling as he strides over to hug Pep Guardiola, Guardiola's not only full of respect but responding warmly; the two coaches discuss things in Spanish before the media arrive.

Guardiola admits that Bielsa just asked him to sum up the match. Admitting "I couldn't do it, he's much cleverer than me and I need time to process what happened", the Catalan, often aggressive particularly with English managers, seems in awe of Marcelo Bielsa's intellect.

A share of the points brings Leeds' total, after four games, to 7 and they stand fifth in the Premiership table. More than that, they've shown they can mix it with mighty Man City!

CHAPTER 3

THE DEMOLITION OF ASTON VILLA

F riday evening October 23 and BT Sport Box Office asking £14.95 for fans to watch Villa versus Leeds, an extortionate charge particularly when you're paying for only a few minutes build up -and worse, no repeats.

BT are full of the Villa who stand in second place having won all four of their games. Of course that includes the 7-2 hammering of Liverpool but that was a freak result stemming from a drastically poor performance by the Reds' reserve keeper plus several others not their usual selves.

Villa manager Dean Smith's a jovial, fair-minded bloke but not the world's greatest tactician. Much of their improvement's down to rigorous defensive drilling by the retired Chelsea hard man John Terry. The main beneficiaries of that are the rugged central defenders Mings and Konsa, one a Southgate regular, the other on the verge of a callup. The media are playing up Chelsea loanee and Everton reject, the chunky, bull-necked Ross Barkley but, for all his strength and shooting power, his reading of the game's not the best. That's something which could never be said about their key man and captain, Jack Grealish. Grealish has made his way into the England squad but is yet to fully convince the obstinate Southgate. Marcelo Bielsa, on the other hand, is only too well aware of the danger Grealish poses and has praised his individual skill. Grealish seems to revel in being BT's focus staring back at the cameras. He's a distinctive figure, long hair thick with gel over his short back and sides with his socks rolled down to his ankles.

Big decisions for Bielsa from the word go. Kalvin Phillips sustained a shoulder injury in the closing minutes of the Wolves game and Liam Cooper's still unavailable. Diego Llorente hasn't recovered from the injury he got on international duty.

Marcelo ingeniously solves his problems by a change of personnel and a redeployment. Luke Ayling, skipper for the day, will play in central defence alongside Robin Koch, Stuart Dallas will switch to right back and Alioski will replace him on the left flank. Pascal Struijk will move forward to defensive midfield where Phillips normally would have played. An imaginative solution typical of Bielsa's agile mind.

Leeds in their classy away kit, dark green shirts with black stripes and yellow epaulettes, kick off with the normally raucous but now empty Holte End at their back. Aston Villa are of course a historic football club, established in 1874 and founder members of the Football League in 1888.Yet their traditional claret and blue kit's now sponsored by car sales website Cazoo.

The media can't resist recalling the famous 2019 match when Marcelo Bielsa won a FIFA fair play award for ordering his men to stand aside and let Villa score after Leeds had exploited a Villa injury to score themselves.

Right from kickoff Leeds are the ones playing football and, in the fourth minute, Harrison, tracking back, gets the better of right back Matty Cash. He looks ahead, sees Alioski free and swiftly plays him in with a pass along the touchline. Alioski's clearly eager to make up for lost time out of the team. The little bleached-blond Macedonian sends a sumptuous early cross into Bamford's path. A diving header from the double-marked Bamford goes just wide and, though BT pundit Robbie Savage calls it a bad miss, that's far too harsh considering Leeds' number 9 was fully 15 yards out when he met the ball. Marcelo Bielsa imperturbably sips coffee seated on his blue throne.

A splendid quickfire passing move from Leeds, Bamford–Harrison–Alioski, the Berkshire boy Cash looks flummoxed at the pressure from the last two, the ball's moved on to Matt Klich, he shapes to shoot from the edge of the box but is strongly tackled out by the sturdy Scotsman John McGinn. McGinn's from Glasgow, a nailed-on Celtic supporter, his grandad was the club chairman.

Villa want it physical and Leeds are ready for them. A full-blooded challenge on the halfway line and Rodrigo knocks down the Brazilian Douglas Luiz. Free kick but Villa can't keep possession so Costa goes on a speedy run down the right all the way to the corner flag only for Barkley to track back and rob him with a rugged challenge.

Leeds are really troubling Villa with their fast paced interchanging. It's just as well for the Brummies that Douglas Luiz intercepts a pass when it seems bound for Bamford.

11 minutes gone and there's trouble for Leeds as soon as Grealish gets into the game. He beats Ayling on the touchline then beats him again as he cuts inside. He's striding through the centre circle in typical style, socks down and shins exposed. Struijk's late with his challenge and sends Grealish sprawling to the turf with a trip. Paul Tierney has no option but to book the Dutchman.

Couple of minutes later and Struijk leaves a trailing leg on Luiz to win the ball and start an attack. Mr Tierney awards Villa a free kick. They want more, they're bawling in vain for Struijk to be sent off. Leeds soon regain possession. Alioski whips in a fine cross for Rodrigo whose header's deflected wide for a corner which the claret and blue crew contrive to clear. It must be said that some referees would have shown Struijk a second yellow. Marcelo Bielsa's frowning and pensive.

It's absolutely all Leeds and Costa breaks free on the right wing and crosses for Rodrigo who's moved cleverly to the near post only to slice his left foot shot across goal and out.

Villa's better players prominent now in both attack and defence; McGinn forces a corner which is well cleared and, as Leeds counter, Douglas Luiz, the dyed-blond carioca, has to make crucial interceptions to foil first Rodrigo then Alioski.

Costa works the right flank where Targett's as badly exposed as is Cash on the other wing. His cross is headed away by Konsa. Rodrigo traps the ball but his intended pass for Bamford's picked up by Villa's Argentinian keeper Martinez. There's danger from Martinez' Route One punt, Grealish's immaculate takedown and first-time flick over Dallas, Robin Koch races over to snuff out the peril with a sturdy tackle, loose ball and Meslier, more or less a spectator so far, collects.

22 minutes and Marcelo makes a decisive substitution. He didn't remove Struijk straightaway after his two fouls in quick succession, he took a little time to think about it but now Struijk's number's up. The risk of him being sent off is clearly enough but how best to replace him, that's the question. Should Stuart Dallas be moved into midfield? Or should Jamie Shackleton go there directly? The Dutchman stalks off expressionless while Shackleton replaces him in midfield. Shackleton looks eager to get on, he knows this is his big chance and he can't wait to take it.

Within two minutes Shackleton shows what he's made of with a perfect pass clipped straight to Dallas' boots. Dallas sees Villa disconcerted and hammers a shot from nearly 30 yards a foot wide of the post.

Leeds are well on top but have to be wary of Jack Grealish. McGinn's long crossfield ball leaves Ayling and Watkins chasing it wide right; Watkins makes up five yards, dodges behind Ayling and fires in a low cross which the hapless Trezeguet scuffs. Grealish pounces on it, pivots and instantly belts a splendid shot beyond

Meslier. Arms upraised to claim the opening goal, Grealish is dumbfounded when Luke Ayling atones for his initial error. He's read the situation perfectly and there he is on the goal line itself to wallop the ball away. Headers from Rodrigo and Shackleton complete the clearance. Goal Decision System indicates that the skipper's rescue act was completed by the narrowest possible margin.

Villa start to make an impact but they're really no match for Leeds. Dallas and Shackleton link up to find Rodrigo only for him to balloon his shot high into the stand. Once again, as against Wolves, Leeds' marvellous approach play is being let down by wayward shooting.

Shackleton's a real live wire and he brings down the vaunted Watkins 30 yards out. It's a foul of course but Savage isn't satisfied it's punishment enough for the Leeds lad. "Shudder been a yeller!" he barks.

A minute before half-time Grealish- played in by Watkins after Koch gave the ball away, dribbles to the edge of the box and goes to ground with a smirk as he brushes past Costa. There's the dreaded VAR decision which, had it gone the wrong way, would have marred the game. Happily there'll be no penalty and Mr Tierney had not been deceived. Grealish is left glowering.

Leeds come close in stoppage time, a wonderfully fluent counter-attack started by Stuart Dallas on the touchline deep in his own half. He floats a long high ball for Rodrigo, the Spaniard instantly taps it to Shackleton who nods it promptly back to him bypassing the desperate Douglas Luiz. A clever pass from Rodrigo to Harrison. He races into a gap where Cash should have been and whips a devastating daisycutter left foot straight into Bamford's path, Bamford's sprinted from the halfway line to get on it, he reaches it ahead of Konsa and Mings only to drive his shot inches wide. Admittedly he might well have scored but Robbie Savage, sounding like a total Bamford sceptic, goes too far, grumbling "'e shudder buried it!"

More than a hint of hostility from the Villa centre backs as the grounded Bamford points an accusatory finger at Konsa. He jumps to his feet and shouts "ref, didn't you see that, he's fouled me!" Yet Mr Tierney has seen nothing and Martinez places a patronising arm round Patrick's shoulder. BT's long camera shot doesn't make it clear whether the centre back stepped on the centre forward or merely stepped round him.

What a marvellous goal it would have been had Patrick Bamford been able to convert that flowing five-man move! Leeds with 60% possession and many more successful passes but nothing to show for it so far.

Second half and Leeds begin where they left off. Rodrigo's having his best game so far and he produces an excellent pass to find Jack Harrison. Harrison motors into the box and shoots wide from an acute angle.

Klich robs the mighty McGinn in the centre circle, goes full steam ahead, finds Rodrigo who prompts Costa, the move looks good but Costa's shot's blocked, rebound to Alioski but he spoons his shot high over.

Sadly it looks like Leeds won't score in a month of Sundays. That's what Jack Grealish thinks and, after robbing Costa deep in his own half, he takes the liberty of embarking on a colossal run, weaving this way and that and tricking his way past every green and black shirt in his path to goal.

It begins after Rodrigo calls for the ball but Costa can only find Matt Targett. Targett's clearance is crap but Costa can only stick out a lazy foot and Grealish disposseses him. With Marcelo Bielsa's angry shouts ringing in his ears, Costa desperately sets off after the Villa star.

Grealish beats Costa a second time then accelerates beyond Klich. Ignoring the unmarked Watkins, he's sure he can do it all on his own anyway. Yes, he's past Koch twice plus Alioski but the big German doesn't give up easy, as he catches up with Grealish the doughty Luke Ayling and the ubiquitous Jamie Shackleton combine to deny him space. Grealish looks pissed off they haven't meekly made way for his magic; he can only stab an angled shot at Meslier who turns it round for a corner.

From Barkley's flag kick, Konsa gets the better of Ayling and lashes a volley on goal. But Illan Meslier's agility incarnate, reacting with a tremendous tip over. That's the mark of a top class keeper–having had little to do but pulling off a supreme save when called into action.

Robbie Savage is in raptures about Grealish going for glory –"it coulda been the goal of the season!" Sure, the Brummie Irish boy's a brilliant player but he's not Maradona or Messi, unless you're at that level football's a passing game. Marcelo Bielsa might well have exempted his two illustrious compatriots had they ever played under him but, were he Grealish's coach, he'd soon school the Brummie boy to consider his teammates and not be greedy for glory.

Immediately afterwards Leeds prove that point with a splendidly worked move which culminates in a ruthless finish. Meslier's kick finds Bamford on the touchline in his own half. As he clips it back to Shackleton, he sets off on a sprint wide right while the move unfolds on the left. Shackleton's too nimble for Barkley, he scoops the ball to Rodrigo, staggers for a moment then recovers to dash forward at speed and act as a decoy while Rodrigo orchestrates the action. Rodrigo Moreno Machado, son of Brazilian football coach Adalberto; his old man would be proud of him now if he saw him cleverly pick out Harrison then race from the halfway line to the edge of the box, full of high-stepping menace. Jack Harrison nonchalantly dummies the hapless Cash and returns the compliment to Rodrigo, John McGinn desperately tries to dispossess Rodrigo but ends up flat on his back as the Spaniard checks his stride before firing in a fierce angled shot. Martinez can only parry it, he lunges after the ball, Mings, caught off balance, urgently tries to bar the path to goal but Patrick Bamford's too quick for him in thought and deed, he rams his shot home from point-blank range.

56 minutes, 0-1 and Bamford's engulfed in wild celebrations led by the excitable Ezgjan plus Raphina rushing on from the sub's quarters. Bielsa signals his stern disapproval. For starters, this is small-time showbiz stuff. What's more, nothing must detract from the concentration required to consolidate the lead.

Signs of instant disarray in the Villa ranks, Barkley shoves Rodrigo down, next the stocky Scouser's whining to the ref after Klich leans on Grealish, he wants the Pole booked but Mr Tierney brushes him aside, next there's trouble in the Villa box, Mings, the 6 foot 5 ex-barman grabs the grounded Bamford by the shirt and drags him up; 'you should be done for diving' so Mings seems to think, scowling at the Leeds' line-leader from below his floppy fringe. On BT Sport they reckon Mings himself is fortunate to escape a yellow.

Had the Holte End been there en masse, they would have been baying for Bamford's blood. As it is, they're reduced to slagging him off on Twitter.

66 minutes, 0-2, Leeds double their lead with a well constructed move superbly finished by Patrick Bamford. Harrison hustles Barkley into a hurried pass which goes straight to Shackleton. Shack finds Klich who's too quick for Barkley, he storms forward, and hangs Douglas Luiz out to dry with a high-speed nutmeg pass to Bamford. Bamford's in the D faced by McGinn and Konsa but they might as well not be there for all they can do. Cushioning the ball with his left foot, using minimal backlift, Bamford arrows an accelerating shot beyond Martinez; it glances the underside of the bar before dropping into the top corner of the net. Martinez stands slack-jawed, awed by Bamford's impudent strike.

Modest celebrations this time, Marcelo Bielsa's made his point. Now he sits on his mobile bucket, his voice resonating round Villa Park as he demands even more.

Villa look unhinged by Leeds' speed and drive, Grealish is booked for a foul on Dallas and mouths off about it in vain to Mr Tierney.

75 minutes, 0-3, Bamford completes his hat-trick in sensational style to climax a splendid five man, seven pass move. Meslier's precise kick to Dallas on the touchline, he shifts it promptly to Shackleton who finds Rodrigo in the centre circle, the Spaniard's delightful 35 yard pass hit with underspin to Costa wide right – Costa to Shackleton and rapid return, Costa's cool square pass to Patrick Bamford waiting on the penalty spot, immediately four Villa defenders cluster menacingly around him. Imperturbable, almost aloof, he traps the ball with the sole of his left foot, then he dances round the rugged Villans jumping away from their boots with his arms lifted up for balance, gliding on to his right with the merest tap of his heel before suddenly twisting to his left and firing a shot into the far corner beyond the keeper's desperate full length dive.

This is a magical, incredible goal. Has Johan Cruyff somehow been reincarnated as Patrick Bamford? Will any of Bamford's detractors ever again dare to argue that he'll never be a top-class striker?

Six minutes later there might well have been a fourth after a floundering Douglas Luiz seemed to handle in the area, VAR ruled that it was unintentional.

Right after that, Bielsa, looking to accustom Raphina to the Premiership in short bursts, brings the Brazilian on to replace Costa. He makes an immediate impact with a masterly diagonal pass which rolls to a stop as perfectly as a wood in a game of crown green bowls, Harrison's on to it at once and squares it for Hernandez, himself an earlier substitute; sadly Pablo slips as he shoots and balloons it over.

There's no letup from Leeds and they're determined to prevent a Villa consolation, so much so that Matt Klich's booked for a foul on McGinn in the buildup; free kick and Ollie Watkins, a pale shadow of the lad the media lauded to high heaven after his performance against a below par Liverpool, can only drag his shot across goal and well wide of the far post.

Mr Tierney adds fully five minutes injury time only protracting Aston Villa's exhaustion as they vainly try to match a far fitter Leeds.

Dean Smith's an honest man and he admits at once that his side were fortunate not to lose by an even bigger margin. Patrick Bamford's interviewed, overjoyed as he's presented with the match ball, he speaks about looking forward to telling his kids all about it one fine day. What a contrast is an openhearted admission like that to MOTD host Gary Lineker and his puerile, carefully rehearsed pun about 'hat-trick Patrick!'

Beyond the totally justified acclaim for Leeds'centre forward, it must be remembered that every single man in a green and black shirt gave a full on brave performance. Luke Ayling skippered the side with immense character and saved the day when Grealish came within an ace of scoring. Jamie Shackleton was a revelation, Illan Meslier was there when he was needed and distributed intelligently in addition to his agility. Above all, Rodrigo looked like a world-class international combining an astute football brain with skilful passing and inexhaustible energy.

As for Patrick Bamford, his delicate footwork must surely have been latent in his earlier years. What he lacked was confidence. Many were biased against him presumably on account of what they perceived as his privileged background. But at the end of the day he showed great character in confronting muscular defenders and maintaining his temper despite taunts. Bamford owes much to Marcelo Bielsa, a coach who describes him as "a noble player", and he's quick to pay tribute to the bosses' guidance.

As for Bielsa's influence on Leeds' performance tonight, this is the way football should be played, boldly adventurous, combining intelligence, skill and formidable fitness, high speed interpassing all culminating in devastating goals.

The Transformation of Thorp Arch

The day after they demolished Aston Villa, the Leeds lads relaxed at their Thorp Arch training ground. It would be 10 days before their next match and preparation for that would start soon enough. In the meantime a mood of justifiable pride gripped the squad. After all, their emphatic victory had come at the expense of the highly rated Birmingham club who'd slaughtered Liverpool 7-2 less than three weeks earlier.

Thorp Arch had been transformed after Marcelo Bielsa's arrival in Leeds. Indeed it had been a condition of his accepting appointment as head coach that this must happen. When Director of Football Victor Orta and CEO Angus Kinnear flew to Buenos Aires to interview him, he outlined his requirements at length.

The new complex must contain a cinema where video footage of upcoming opponents would be analysed in depth and every man in the team would become thoroughly familiar with the style of play of whoever he would be tasked with marking.

With the mental side of the game taken care of, physical conditioning would become paramount. But it was not only the hyper demanding non-stop action so-called 'murder ball' sessions that featured. Diet became ultra-important and every day began with players being weighed and their weight compared to previous readings. There would be no chance to hide the merest hint of flab from the calipers wielded by the physios.

Training was of course on an all day basis. No more could a player expect to casually complete a couple of hours of kickabout before clearing off to play golf and fritter the rest of the day away. The culture of Leeds United fundamentally changed.

In no way was the new Thorp Arch a Spartan camp or some sort of dreaded infringement on a footballer's liberty. Far from it, it became a home from home for them all. In the games room they could hone their competitive instincts in table tennis or snooker. Tired muscles would be revived in the swimming pool. Players cracked jokes as they reclined on fitness machines waiting for their turn with the masseurs.

Now one thing that was notable about the Leeds squad was the genuine friendliness between the lads. There were other Premiership teams where barely concealed resentment simmered below the surface. Yet whether the camaraderie at Thorp Arch was just a happy accident or whether Victor Orta's meticulously compiled recruitment dossiers contained personality profiles wasn't clear.

What was patently obvious was that the Leeds lads loved Thorp Arch. Above all it provided them with the superb physical conditioning which translated itself into a joy in performance on match day. Bielsa's methods were perfectly summed up by the Spanish international Ander Herrera who knew them from the inside during his time at Athletic Bilbao. Said Herrera "Marcelo Bielsa's very demanding in terms of cardio capacity." He added that he'd "seen some players coming off the training pitch vomiting and absolutely exhausted. But when you play the next game, you feel like you're flying – you're absolutely flying!"

CHAPTER 4
NEWCASTLE GET A GOOD HIDING

On December 16 Newcastle arrive at Elland Road. Lying one place ahead of Leeds in mid-table, they're without two unnamed players still struggling in their recovery from Covid. Leeds unchanged-with the vital caveat that Rodrigo too is suffering from Long Covid and this is only his second start in nearly two months.

This match is a significant milestone for Marcelo Bielsa, his 114th game in charge of Leeds United-now exceeding the total he had when coaching Athletic Bilbao, the longest previous spell in his managerial career. Asked about it in interview, he replies, speaking through his interpreter as usual, that he's very happy to remain at Leeds.

Pre-match top-class ex-strikers from either side, Jimmy Hasselbaink and Les Ferdinand are asked to discuss the respective merits of Patrick Bamford and Callum Wilson, Hasselbaink prefers Wilson, Ferdinand succinctly sums up the case against Wilson "he has to be fed, Bamford doesn't."

Up and running, Luke Ayling hits a very good long ball to Alioski on the wing, he passes to Harrison who forces a corner, from the corner Cooper's header's parried by Darlow, Raphina moves in but is quickly closed down.

Ciaran Clark's long ball forward, passing to Wilson, Dallas keeps Wilson at bay, there's a loose ball, Fraser shoots, Meslier parries, Alioski stabs it clear, Newcastle can't follow-up.

0-1 at the second attempt –in the 26th minute-the black shirted Geordies succeed, Dallas isn't tight on Fraser, Fraser swoops on the ball, hits a classic cross to the near post, Wilson nods on and Alioski's slow to react at the far post, enabling the long-haired, bushy- bearded Irishman Hendricks to crash the ball home.This was poor collective defence fom Leeds; Dallas(unusually), Ayling-who couldn't cope with Wilson-and Alioski all at fault.

Ryan Fraser's a remarkable player, but at only 5'4" the diminutive Aberdonian scarcely seems to have the stature to be a professional footballer but he compensates for it with elegant ball control and astute intelligence. He's a favourite with thinking Magpies.

Leeds, undaunted, press forward, one or two strange decisions from the tubby, shaven- headed ref Simon Hooper but he'll soon be right on the ball with the big one.

Just turned the half hour, Alioski to Harrison, his good cross, Raphina shoots with strength but mis-hits it giving Darlow the chance to parry before his defenders kick the ball clear.

1-1, 35, Dallas in the centre circle plays a neat pass to Bamford standing with his back to goal, Bamford patiently plays an angled pass back to Klich who sweeps the ball wide to Raphinha in space moving in with a menacing stride, Rodrigo calls for the ball and Raphinha delivers an impeccable hanging cross for Rodrigo who's cleverly got between the two centre backs, Darlow's come out a shade too far, Rodrigo deliberately loops a header over him, it strikes the bar but drops for Bamford, cool as you please, to nod down and in, Bamford's ninth of the season, albeit only his second at Elland Road. Though the finish was simple Bamford had been anticipating cleverly all the while.

Leeds' goal is the result of their incisive passing and ability to instantly change the focus of attack. Parity at half-time but you ain't seen nothing yet.

Early in the second half a controversial penalty decision, Lewis makes good progress down the left, he crosses low beyond Ayling, Wilson and Cooper tussle for the ball, Wilson falls and appeals for the spot kick, Mr Hooper turns it down and VAR confirms his decision.

Newcastle's burly, battle-scarred manager Steve Bruce is furious, yet the replay shows that Cooper actually got the side of his heel on the ball, minimal contact certainly but contact it is nevertheless.

An hour gone and Leeds go ahead, 2-1, following superb play by two men, Rodrigo Moreno and Jack Harrison, Rodrigo's calm chest trap of a high ball, then he shakes off his marker, pivots and picks out Harrison with a splendidly struck left foot cross, Harrison's full stretch toe trap, then he confidently takes the ball right up to the byline before he delivers a lovely dipping cross on the half turn for Rodrigo, Rodrigo's great diving header from 10 yards out brilliantly angled just inside the post.

Rodrigo and Harrison hug, Brazilian-born Spanish international and American-educated Englishman perfectly on the same wavelength.

Leeds, boosted by this move right out of the top drawer, surge back into attack, Cooper's long ball, turned by Klich into Bamford's path, Bamford gets beyond Clark, he shoots, Darlow does very well to dive on it at the base of the post and scoop it round for a corner.

Sadly that corner only leads indirectly to a counter-attacking Newcastle goal, Phillips trying to play it back on the ground to a teammate finds the sturdy Scotsman Fraser instead who runs forward strongly and delivers a pass into Murphy's path, Murphy's good low cross looking for Wilson, Wilson was caught in mid stride but manages to get a shot on target only for Meslier to tip it over.

From the corner, more set piece woe, Clark leaps clear above Ayling and heads an unstoppable shot past Meslier, 75 minutes gone, 2-2. It doesn't make sense, it's totally against the run of play, Newcastle aren't on the map with Leeds for football but they've put the ball in the net twice. Luke Ayling was badly at fault here, barely managing to get off the ground.

With fifteen minutes remaining, Bruce strangely removes his cleverest player, Fraser.

Shortly afterwards Leeds, showing total belief, regain the lead, Harrison races in and robs Sean Longstaff, then he calmly drops back, plays in Bamford in the box and moves off right, bemusing the Newcastle defence, yet Bamford, double marked, keeps the defenders guessing before he opts to pass wide left to Klich, Klich crosses to the far post over the heads of Raphina and his marker, Newcastle slip up badly because no one's tracked Stuart Dallas and with a stooping header he rams the high bouncing ball powerfully home from close range.

This looks as if it might be decisive, Steve Bruce pulls a face, Marcelo Bielsa's inscrutable, pensive, he makes two substitutions in quick succession, Rodrigo goes off, he's made a wonderful contribution but he's tiring after his effort, so the wily veteran Hernandez replaces him, Pablo's wearing black gloves against the cold, as is the youthful Tyler Roberts replacing Bamford.

Newcastle pressing strongly in the closing stages for an equaliser which never comes, quite the opposite with five minutes remaining it's 4-2, Phillips relatively subdued until now after a booking launches a counter-attack with a fine 25 yard pass to Raphina, Raphina breaks away with a raking stride, dawdles momentarily toying with the defender then finds Roberts fresh and sprinting alongside him, Newcastle are completely undone by the pace and panache of it all, Leeds had 5 men flooding forward against two defenders, Roberts passes shrewdly for Klich but, with Alioski racing up behind him yelling "leave it to me!", the Pole defers, leaving the little Balkan extravert to thump the ball home-a relatively simple task to finish an excellent team goal.

87 minutes, the icing on the cake, from Murphy's corner, Dallas heads the ball down to Hernandez wide left but unmarked, Hernandez finds Jack Harrison with a brilliant 20 yard pass, this is the signal for Harrison to deliver a great individual goal, picking the pass up lying deeper than the centre circle, he might have passed back to the also breaking Klich but decides to go it alone; he heads off on a wonderful weaving, jinking run, draws two defenders towards him and dodges them as if they weren't there. Then comes the piece de resistance-a fulminating 30 yard shot high into the top corner, an absolute living flame. Keeper Darlow can only stare at him in horrified disbelief.

On the touchline Marcelo Bielsa celebrates jubilantly, springing to his feet and punching the air with both fists. The victory was wrapped up anyway but this is a wonderful goal for Leeds, Bielsa is a connoisseur of goals, he's seen many a beautiful strike in his time but probably few better than this thunderbolt from Jack Harrison. Harrison's shooting power rests in his heavy thighs, his skill and football brain seem innate.

Bruce is grudging in defeat, not a word of praise for Leeds-only maintaining that "we gave three poor goals away, the third, the fourth and the fifth" but in actual fact his team only slipped up for the third, no blame could reasonably have been attached to Newcastle for the last two when, tired out by Leeds' irresistible attacking and far superior fitness, they were unable to prevent first an excellent team goal then Harrison's world-class strike.

On MOTD, there's the usual prattle about 'Leeds the entertainers' and a bland comment from Danny Murphy that "at this rate they're not going to be involved in a relegation battle." Then there's a long discussion of the penalty incident. Micah Richards naïvely observes "as a defender I'm always going to say it is one-"

following which Lineker concludes with the absurd remark "Slo-mo distorts a lot of things."

Beyond the margin of victory, only the second at home so far, one very significant thing is that there were five different scorers. No longer reliant on Patrick Bamford, Dallas and Alioski weighed in too and both Rodrigo and, even more so, Harrison produced exceptional strikes.

Rodrigo, still suffering from his illness, is a very intelligent player, well capable of orchestrating moves. Jack Harrison, after an inexplicable dip in form, reminds us all of his tremendous talent. And Newcastle United have been given a proper good hiding!

In his postmatch interview Marcelo Bielsa resiled from the slightest exultation, instead admitting that that his team had conceded twice from set plays. He pointed to this weakness as the major cause of four defeats in the previous six games. He noted, however, that his central defenders were disadvantaged by lack of height against the attackers with whom they duelled. He refrained from saying, as most other coaches in his situation undoubtedly would have, that both the central defenders Leeds had purchased – Robin Koch and Diego Llorente –had been plagued with injury.

In contrast to Steve Bruce's churlishness, Marcelo Bielsa remained dignified at all times.

Bielsa's damning indictment of media mischief

Four days after Newcastle were routed, Leeds suffered their heaviest defeat of the season, losing 6-2 to Manchester United at Old Trafford. In the aftermath of this loss, media criticism of Marcelo Bielsa mounted exponentially and, four days after the match, Bielsa held a press conference at Thorp Arch to answer his critics.

From the start, his body language was different from his usual posture. Looking the assembled throng straight in the eye whilst glancing from time to time at a dossier he'd compiled, he was of course obliged to rely on Andres Clavijo for translation. Had Clavijo interpreted more vibrantly, Bielsa's indictment of media mischief would doubtless have been even more damning.

Bielsa opened his attack with the observation that the media had made no attempt to analyse the result and could only assert that Leeds' style must be promptly changed. He went on to say that the media were incapable of looking beyond results. "Whenever there's adversity, what you people do is to further weaken those who are suffering the adversity and to ridicule the style of play of a team."

Without specifically naming Gary Lineker on Twitter, he referred to a comment that Leeds' style of play was attractive- especially to their opponents! Some voices were, he noted, capable of analysing beyond the results but most were not. What worried him about this was that it decreased the public's capacity to understand and sought to destabilise by suggesting to the players that the style needed to be changed.

As far as the match at Old Trafford was concerned, Leeds were superior to United in the physical aspect even though United exceeded their previous peak of physicality. Leeds were superior in possession whilst domination fluctuated throughout the game.

What swung the game in United's favour was the way in which their manager deployed two midfielders, Fred and McTominay. He admitted that he hadn't thought the key to the game would lie with those two players.

Bielsa went on to state that whereas Leeds had created more chances, namely eleven, they'd only scored twice whereas United with only eight chances had scored six times.

Marcelo went on to argue that, as always, the media wanted Leeds to abandon imagination in the short-term quest for results. While he was coaching Leeds in the Championship, for the most part everything went well and the media were quiet. Yet even then if there was any brief turbulence the press demanded immediate change.

Referring to criticism that Leeds were still chasing the game even in the last few minutes despite being four goals down, Bielsa said that he would have liked to reduce the margin of painful defeat even at the risk of conceding a further goal. In essence the game turned on Leeds' inability to score from all out attacking in contrast to United's capacity to get goals from counter-attacks.

Bielsa poured scorn on the notion that he prioritised style ahead of results; an attacking mode might lead to reverses in the short run but it would only be by maintaining it regardless of criticism that the Leeds players would reach their full potential in terms of results.

Marcelo Bielsa had remained objective throughout his response. Undoubtedly he'd been angered by media mischief in the aftermath of the defeat but, at Thorp Arch, he sublimated this into a devastating forensic indictment whilst admitting to an error of judgement over the two Manchester midfielders.

In their reaction to his conference, certain media elements were incorrigible, the Daily Mail absurdly referring to what he said as "a rant." Gary Lineker, who'd tweeted 'Leeds fun to watch and fun to play against' made no further comment, almost certainly fearful of challenging a man of Bielsa's intellect.

Leeds' players had never wavered in their support for their coach. Questioned about it, Patrick Bamford spoke for the team when he said "we're all right behind him, a hundred per cent."

The best thing of all was the continuing total support of Leeds fans. They were quick to counter all the deplorable nonsense on social media with Graham Winstanley retorting to Lineker's tweet with the words "tell that to Newcastle, Everton and Villa" while Courtines in his tweet noted that Leeds "were playing a full-back at centre back and half the team are from the Championship. They're doing great!"

In the Telegraph James Ducker, under the crude headline 'Ole Gunnar Solskjaer did a number on Marcelo Bielsa', had laid into Bielsa, absurdly comparing him to Kevin Keegan and sneering that he'd never won anything outside his native Argentina. According to him, Bielsa "must have had a death wish coming to Old Trafford" and producing "90 crackpot minutes."

Many readers were rightly scornful of Ducker's assertions for various reasons. The most telling was Chris Harvey's retort that "Manchester United's squad cost a combined total of £628.1 million in transfer fees, Leeds £120.3 million. It would be fairer to compare what the results said about the two managers if Bielsa had another 500 million to spend and United put out a set of players who cost the same amount."

CHAPTER 5

OUTCLASSING CLASSY LEICESTER

Leeds visited the King Power Stadium in the early afternoon of January 31 to face Leicester riding high in third position but weakened by the absence of star striker Jamie Vardy. His replacement, Ayoze Pérez is nowhere near the same quality. That said, Vardy's goalscoring had dropped off at Christmas before he was obliged to have a hernia operation. In his absence attacking midfielders James Maddison, Harvey Barnes and Youri Tielemans had regularly scored and Leicester were unbeaten in seven games.

Having crossed swords with two of the foremost European coaches, Juergen Klopp and Pep Guardiola, Marcelo Bielsa found himself facing Brendan Rodgers, by far the best British manager. Certain journalists had been openly sceptical about what they called 'the Bielsa myth' when Leicester had beaten Leeds 4-1 in the reverse fixture. They pointed to Rodgers' cautious counter-attacking strategy, asserting that it had nullified Leeds' all out attacking. In actual fact Bielsa had been badly let down on the day by a series of defensive errors from Cooper, Klich, Koch and even Dallas.

Brendan Rodgers' highly impressive managerial career had been marked by a studious approach unusual among British managers. After his playing career was prematurely cut short by injury, he studied the methods of the finest coaches in Spain, becoming fluent in Spanish. Appointed assistant coach by Jose Mourinho at Chelsea, he then went on to achieve success with lower division clubs culminating in winning promotion to the Premiership for cash-strapped Welsh outsiders Swansea City. He was then appointed manager of Liverpool and in 2013-14 the Reds seemed poised to win the Premiership title before being narrowly pipped by Manchester City with two games remaining.

After Liverpool decided to dispense with his services, Rodgers went to Celtic where he achieved an astonishing 69.8% win ratio in two and a half seasons. Meanwhile his successor at Anfield, Klopp, benefited hugely from Rodgers' astute signings notably Brazilians Roberto Firmino and Philippe Coutinho.

Tempted south by Leicester, Rodgers at once revitalised Jamie Vardy's career which had seemed to be in permanent decline. Now Brendan seemed faintly surprised by the warmth of Marcelo's greeting, arm on shoulder in friendly acknowledgment of his rival's achievements.

Today Marcelo Bielsa's relying on Liam Cooper and Pascal Struijk as his central defenders and Mateusz Klich is benched for the second successive match.

Sky are giving the game prime TV coverage but veteran pundit Graeme Souness unwisely remarks that Bielsa seems more concerned about Leeds' performance than about winning matches. Clearly he hadn't taken on board Jermaine Beckford's prior observation that Leeds have been weakened by injuries to three of their four centre backs. Souness seemed entrenched in his partially deprecating view that "Leeds are the great entertainers." Whereas Jamie Redknapp notes that Bamford hasn't scored for four games, Beckford remarked that Patrick has much more to his game than goals alone. He also pointed out the distance Leeds cover in game after game and singled out Jack Harrison in particular for his "phenomenal workrate."

The match begins with a foul by Alioski who's troubled by the underrated winger Albrighton. James Maddison takes the free-kick, his face a mask of concentration under his carefully brushed back hair and baked-in frown. He looks to catch out Meslier with a direct chip only to see his effort sail over. His centre backs look reproachfully at him denying them the chance to test what they think is Leeds' suspect defence.

In the eighth minute Leeds mount a sparkling counter-attack which might well have led to a goal; when Albrighton tries to dribble into the box, Cooper foils him with a splendid sliding tackle and, from the floor, he deftly prods the ball forward to Dallas who steers a pinpoint pass to Bamford, Bamford neatly turns the ball back to Phillips, Phillips' first-time pass to Rodrigo; Rodrigo springs Leeds into all out assault as he sweeps a perfect pass to the unmarked Raphinha on the right flank, James Justin desperately tries to stem the flow but by now Raphinha's delivered a fine chip into Bamford's path, Bamford shows he's right on his game again with a nifty takedown and turn laying the ball off to Harrison, Jack squares it to Stuart Dallas and Stuart nutmegs Fofana even as he passes beyond Castaigne. For the moment it looks like the perfect preamble to a goal with Bamford having only the keeper to beat from 10 yards, yet Dallases' radar's slightly off, it's a stride beyond the centre forward before it goes out of play.

Leicester have been reduced to statues by Leeds breathlessly chipping and stroking the ball about at high speed, only a marginal error precluded what would have been a wonderful goal, the culmination of a nine pass move involving seven men. Leeds in their pristine white shirts look like Real Madrid of yesteryear suddenly translated into the 21st-century, running like Olympic 400 metre men.

With Phillips hard at work in the engine room, tough tackling and resolute, the Peacocks look certain to seize the lead —only to be hit by a splendid Leicester goal which would have jolted the confidence of a lesser side.

In the 12th minute Cooper's ambitious long ball swung out towards the touchline for Raphinha is intercepted by Justin who promptly finds Harvey Barnes. Barnes has become a goal menace second only to the absent Vardy. As skilful as he's sturdy, full of dash and panache, he bursts clean through the middle with Luke Ayling at fault for not getting tight to him. Try as he might, Ayling can't close the gap, Barnes and Maddison brilliantly swap passes and Barnes finishes in sensational style, trapping Maddison's sharply angled return with a fantastic double touch and swerving at top speed before clipping it far beyond Meslier.

Harvey Barnes, the 23-year-old local lad from suburban Countesthorpe, freshfaced and exuberant, jumps for joy, the prime mover in a truly great goal.

Utterly undaunted, Leeds equalize within two minutes. The usually precise Maddison underhits a pass and Ayling intercepts it with a confident grin before racing forward along the touch-line. Bamford's drifted clear of Leicester's much-vaunted youthful French centre back Wesley Fofana and Dallas has surged forward in the prime of his fitness and ground covering. Found by Luke, Pat Bamford rolls the ball into Stuart Dallases' path with an immaculately dainty little pass and, from a wide angle, the battling Ulsterman cracks it past Schmeichel.

Even Marcelo Bielsa's surprised by the suddenness of the riposte. Jumping up to acclaim it, he spills some of his coffee on his tunic and hastily wipes it off. He's not content with parity. "Need more!" he shouts —"play!!"

A couple of Leicester players look rattled by the Whites' retort, none more so than the Belgian Timothy Castaigne who's looked uncomfortable against Harrison from kick-off.

Everything was going swimmingly for Leeds until Rodrigo, dodging cleverly round the back of Fofana and stretching to trap a misplaced pass from Alioski-who was bent on a flying nutmeg against Pappy Mendy- slumps to the turf holding his groin. Bielsa and Quiroga confer anxiously as the physios attend to the stricken Spaniard. He seems to recover, stretches vigorously on the touch-line and jogs back to the fray.

Leicester think they've grabbed the lead back when Barnes pounces on a poor clearance from Struijk and once again swaps passes with Maddison who prompts Perez, the Spaniard duly nets but has clearly strayed offside, flagged instantly by the ponytailed ref's assistant Sian Massey- Ellis.

Meanwhile Rodrigo's down again and there's no alternative but to substitute him. Klich's briefed at length by Bielsa.

Kalvin Phillips almost effortlessly delivers a high pinpoint pass to Raphinha but it's charged down before he can take decisive action. Leeds have a clear majority of possession, 62%.

26 minutes and Bamford calls for a cross from Harrison, it's slightly deflected thus confusing Schmeichel, Bamford makes a huge leap but Leicester's keeper re-adjusts and grabs the ball just under the crossbar.

On the half-hour Klich- who's clearly noted Bielsa's instructions- suddenly switches play with a long, high-bouncing crossfield ball which finds Harrison well clear of Castaigne. Harrison shoots on the run with a left foot volley so powerful that Schmeichel's driven to the floor as he pushes it behind for a corner. From the corner, cleverly flighted by Phillips, it's Leeds' turn to have a goal disallowed. Bamford outjumps Jonny Evans with ease and the ball flies goalwards off the side of his head. Somehow Kasper Schmeichel manages to get his gloves on it. Referee Chris Kavanagh hears no sound on his GDS watch and Schmeichel's incredible point blank save rebounds to Klich with the keeper grounded. Klich kicks it into the net from close range. The Pole's offside, however, a decision –even though Bamford chooses to harangue the ref about it –which is as accurate as the previous one against Perez.

Leeds force Schmeichel into a further desperate save after a fine close passing move. Ayling begins it with a ball to Raphinha who nonchalantly nutmegs Mendy to find Klich. Klich returns the compliment and Raphinha bursts past Evans laying it off to Bamford, the brilliant Brazilian instantly kills Bamford's return and blasts a shot on goal which Schmeichel somehow manages to turn round for a corner.

You can't help but acknowledge Kasper Schmeichel's great goalkeeping. The big blond Dane may have spent an unhappy year at Elland Road but he's since become a splendid shot stopper.

Though the corner's cleared, Brendan Rodgers stands lips pursed in his technical zone looking a worried man. It's not just that Leeds are attacking with brio-he'd reckoned on that but not with their defensive stability, when Albrighton beats Harrison and swerves away from Cooper to find Barnes who returns the compliment, it looks as if Leicester might score but Meslier parries the winger's shot and Struijk thunders the ball clear. As for the sulking Spaniard Pérez, he doesn't look as if he fancies mixing it with Liam Cooper.

With 10 minutes left before halftime, Rodgers turns to the excellent Portuguese full-back Ricardo Pereira. Ricardo's only in the early stages of his comeback after spending 10 months on the sidelines with a cruciate ligament injury. When Castaigne's duly subbed, it's stated that he's sustained a knock–possibly he has yet he was struggling against Harrison since kickoff. What's more, he just rowed angrily with his surly teammate Fofana tapping his forehead to suggest the Frenchman's slow thinking had left him having to cope with a dangerous Ayling cross.

Leeds continue to press on and Sky's Jamie Carragher, who's seen all the best European sides during his time as a Liverpool central defender, shrewdly comments "you can only marvel at some o'

Leeds moves –tell you what, the TV screen doesn't really capture 'em, yer 'ave to see 'em for yerself !"

Ayling's booking by Mr Kavanagh leads to Barneses' shot which loops up high, the whistle goes for Fofana's foul on Cooper even before Maddison blasts the dropping ball against the bar.

Fofana's looking distinctly disgruntled but the ex-Man U veteran Evans is struggling just as much as him to cope with Bamford's clever movements.

Suddenly Meslier, far less busy than Schmeichel during the entire half, is called into action after an excellent through ball from Albrighton seeks out Maddison at the far post but the young Frenchman dives on it in the nick of time with Cooper standing guard.

A truly absorbing 45 minutes of football ends on a note of comedy when the baby-faced Belgian Tielemans' exaggerated scream as Alioski clips his ankles is ignored by Ms Massey- Ellis even though she has a ringside view of their ignoble encounter.

It's half-time in the Sky studio and Souness is clearly taken aback by the power of Leeds' performance; he seeks an explanation insinuating that Leicester have not been pulling their weight, being overconfident after their 4-1 victory at Elland Road.

On the resumption Brendan Rodgers' strategic change is unveiled, he's withdrawn Albrighton and introduced the Turk, Kaglar Soyuncu, to complete a three man defensive back line, the thing is that Soyuncu's a better distributor than either Evans or Fofana and Rodgers will expect him to sortie into midfield.

Leicester are clearly looking up and Justin and Ricardo combine menacingly, Struijk coolly concedes a corner to avert the danger, in actual fact there's two successive corners from which nothing comes, Leicester's only hope is an appeal to VAR after Fofana falls flat in a tussle with Cooper, VAR dismisses the penalty claim, quite right too because the French lad simply lacked the weight to go shoulder to shoulder with the Whites' skipper.

Next thing Luke Ayling's grinning imperturbably as Stuart Dallas tells him there's a smear of blood on his forehead, the rugged geezer never felt a thing but now Mr Kavanagh orders him to the sideline to get his napper wrapped up in a bandage.

Bielsa has had a word with Illan Meslier and the keeper starts hurling the ball long distance to initiate Whites' counters. What's more, Marcelo's shouting revised instructions about man-to-man marking in light of Rodgers' redeployment. When Alioski pushes Ricardo down that's not what the manager meant and Rodgers swings up his arms in protest; Mr Kavanagh declines to take action.

Things are not going so well for Leeds now, Stuart Dallas is following instructions to the letter but, obliged to keep an eye on Maddison, he can't drive forward the way he was doing in the first half. Alioski, for his part, is slow to readjust and constantly dragged out of position. The wind's been taken out of Leeds' sails.

Can the Peacocks be physically rugged? You bet they can, Perez is whining about Struijk's tough tackling and Dallas is booked for tripping Tielemans. 20 minutes gone in the second half and this is what Leeds are relying on, precluded from resuming their adventurous attacks. When Maddison find Pérez, Struijk robs him and, even though he slips in doing so, Cooper completes the clearance.

In the 70th minute Leeds spark back to life with a splendid goal. Ricardo fails to trap Evans' clumsy clearance only diverting the ball into midfield. Struijk seizes the chance, brushes Perez aside and passes to Raphina who instantly glides a perfect pass to Bamford's boots, Bamford swerves imperiously past Soyuncu and fires a ferocious shell of a shot over Schmeichel's head to glance off the underside of the bar and explode in the far side of the net.

Jamie Carragher sums up succinctly "no goalkeeper in the world's savin' that!"

The South Americans in the Peacocks' technical zone are jubilant – Pablo Quiroga crushes the air downwards with both fists,

Diego Flores pumps an elbow; "Golazo!" they shout while Marcelo Bielsa mimics a deadly karate chop.

Yes, Leeds have regained the lead, but Bielsa, regaining his calm, wants no time wasted on premature celebration –"still need more!" he reminds them.

Mat Klich, not to be outdone in the ruggedness stakes, goes in studs first on Pappy Mendy, leaving the chubby little Frenchman howling in pain. Out comes Mr Kavanagh's yellow card for Leeds' third booking, then there's a free kick which Leeds fail to clear, Fofana swings a boot, Cooper looks to block and it ricochets off his shoulder high over the bar. From the corner Soyuncu makes a titanic leap and heads the ball down towards the far post. Jonny Evans races in for the kill only to be impeded by the feckless Pérez. The furious ex-Old Trafford merchant has to pull up sharp to avoid ramming his crotch against the goalpost.

Leicester had come within inches of an equaliser and Marcelo Bielsa will not be content till his lads score again –"keep going forward TO WIN THEES GAME!!!" His voice booms round the desolate King Power Stadium.

At this stage Rodgers seeks to ensure that Leeds don't do just that by withdrawing the scowling Fofana and sending on Genghis Under, Soyuncu's compatriot, the very man who'd slotted home decisively for the Foxes at Elland Road.

Perez, seeking to atone for his earlier error, unleashes a fiery snapshot but Meslier pulls off an excellent save.

Now it's sad to see that Bielsa has to replace Raphinha who's gone down with what looks like a thigh strain. He's obliged to draft in Helder Costa with a quarter of an hour left and Costa contributes little.

Leeds are doing exactly what the boss told them, they force a corner and a Sky commentator wrongly claims "Struijk could have scored from 3 yards there but all he's done is an air kick." A minute later his skipper Liam Cooper asks him "how close was that, Paz?"

Struijk responds with a gesture indicating a stud's length, Sky are obliged to replay the incident and, true enough, Struijk was only foiled at the last split-second by the studs of Ricardo's boots.

83 minutes and Costa foolishly fouls Maddison, presenting Leicester with a clear chance to equalise but what happens is a wonderful Leeds' counter-attack and the deciding goal. It begins with Struijk who heads the ball carefully out to Klich, Dallas takes over, he beats two Leicester men, dumping one down to the ground with a meaty shoulder charge and passes down the line to Klich; and it's the Pole who spies Patrick Bamford breaking menacingly still in his own half, he finds him at once and Bamford sprints forward, Leicester have been cut to ribbons by the speed and precision of it all and only Schmeichel stands between Bamford and a certain goal.

As Bamford reaches the box, Evans has nearly caught up with him but all the while Jack Harrison's been making a parallel run, beginning 10 yards behind but now level. In a touch which combines unselfishness with tactical savvy, Bamford squares the ball and Harrison boots it home from eight yards.

Harrison smiles broadly as he points to Bamford, they swap high fives and hug. The whole team's lit up and Marcelo Bielsa has what he was looking for, a two goal lead. He flails both fists in satisfaction, yelling "GOL" and "YES!!" Still he encourages the lads – "Come on! Get on this ball!!" But Brendan Rodgers is tightlipped, he knows his boys have been done for on their own ground.

In the Sky studio Souness still hasn't caught up with it all, he prattles on about Leeds being "gung ho." The other pundits focus on Bamford's unselfishness. He's rightly picked out for praise having scored one goal and assisted two, so is Raphina for his brilliant assist for Bamford's goal, not a word said about the invisible man Struijk, the burly Dutchman who was not only a defensive barrier but was also the first mover for both the second and third goals, they couldn't spell his surname for toffee, they don't have to do but they can't pronounce it either. Truly Pascal is an unsung hero.

In the post match interview Laura Woods smiles charmingly as she starts to question Marcelo Bielsa. She gets a brief smile out of him before he proceeds to give his analysis of the match in which he praises Leicester as excellent opponents before going on to remark that Patrick Bamford's a player who always puts his team before himself.

This victory is a significant milestone for Leeds –the first time they've beaten a top four Premiership side. They'd drawn with Manchester City, lost narrowly to Liverpool and have been crushed 6-2 by Manchester United, in a match where the margin of defeat exaggerated the Mancs' actual superiority on the day.

Whilst all three goals were excellent, the Whites' increased defensive solidity was notable. Above all, Marcelo Bielsa's ability to counteract Brendan Rodgers' astute half-time tactical changes was vital as was his constant encouragement of his Leeds lads, urging them on to higher and higher peaks of achievement.

BT Sport Question Bielsa

Before covering Leeds' away game against Manchester City, BT Sport broadcast what it claimed was an interview with Marcelo Bielsa. In fact Bielsa does not grant interviews and, so far from departing from his usual practice, he'd simply permitted BT Sport to put questions of their choosing to him. His answers were written on screen beside his talking head. They were given in Spanish with no interpreter present and an agreed translation made.

The questions were preceded by remarks from two Leeds players about Bielsa's personality.

Patrick Bamford said "ultimately he's just a guy who really loves football" and Rodrigo commented "he's like a scientist, he analyses everything."

BT Sport's questions appeared in random order. In the first instance Bielsa replied to a question which didn't appear on screen and might have been vague. He said "I always try to focus on what's to come rather than what's already been done" adding "football is something you can't predict –and that's what makes it so attractive."

Asked why he thought so many neutrals enjoyed watching Leeds, he answered "our admirers aren't Leeds' fans who are happy if Leeds win and sad if they lose-which is the case for all Leeds' fans. These admirers are freer to judge the beauty of what they are watching."

Asked for his opinion of the Premiership, Bielsa replied "the Premiership's a place where the most important thing is what happens on the pitch and that's something which is losing importance in the world today." He elaborated –"everywhere else the happenings off the pitch seem to be a way of stoking up interest in fans using things which are worthless." Even so, "in England there's still the desire to look at the game only."

Questioned about what the future might hold for him (a subject of immense interest to all Leeds' fans with Bielsa's contract not yet finalized) he responded "I'm really grateful to have been accepted in the three years I've been here." Steering away from a direct answer, he continued "you should think about the future when the time is right" adding "there are two main factors –the footballers who are responsible for your ideas coming to fruition or not and the fans who judge them."

BT Sport made no attempt to analyse what Bielsa had said and swiftly moved on to other matters, leaving viewers free to draw their own conclusions.

Looking at Marcelo Bielsa's observations in order, he began, consciously or otherwise, by separating himself from commentators who continually bang on about the past, above all in reference to Leeds' tribulations during their 16 year exile from the Premiership. What's more, he was implicitly brushing aside pundits' penchant for negative forecasts –the likes of "what d'you reckon, Gary?" and replies such as "Leeds'll score, yeah, but they'll always concede more than they score."

Regarding the differing reactions of Leeds' supporters and neutral aficionados, it seemed clear that Bielsa loved the fans for their unshakeable joy and pride whilst at the same time stressing that football was a beautiful game when played in an adventurous manner.

His condemnation of events off the pitch appeared to be a veiled attack on social media trolling and mischievous transfer speculation. These of course are rife in England yet Bielsa may have experienced them as far worse while coaching in other countries.

Finally, he showed his humility in appreciation of the love he received in the city of Leeds. Rather than the slightest hint of boasting about his transformation of the club, he preferred to praise the players who put his ideas and methods into practice. For him there would never be the equation 'Bielsa=Leeds' but always the acknowledgement that his brilliant lads were partners in what had been accomplished and that, above all, it was the verdict of the Whites' fans which needed to be respected.

CHAPTER 6

WHEN TEN MEN BEAT MAN CITY TWO ONE

It had been snowing in Manchester on the morning of the 10th April but Leeds had brought the sun with them and, despite the bitter cold, it's brilliantly sunny for the midday kick-off.

The match is being televised by BT Sport and, before it starts, their anchorman Jake Humphrey asks two pundits how far Leeds can go under Bielsa with his style. The pair are Rio Ferdinand and the ex-Manchester City central defender Joleon Lescott. Lescott's the first to answer. "They're close to a ceiling" he asserts, continuing "in the Championship they had players who were better than their opponents nine times out of ten. But when you come up to this level –we're talking world-class players –they're not going on to become a European side, a Champions League side with this style of play."

Ferdinand takes his turn. "It comes down to recruitment" he insists, going on to say "are you going to buy players at a better level who are going to adhere to your methods? I mean the intensity of the training, it's gruelling and there are not a lot of players that can benefit from it that would actually want to do it. You could do it but would you want to do it every day in training? It's hard!"

Lescott has another bite at the cherry. He says "I've never heard anyone discredit Bielsa and any player who leaves Leeds will have been improved by working with him but if players are losing by four or five goals and defenders are getting abused, that must be hard for them to take." Ferdinand agrees, claiming that "against the lesser teams they've fared very well but when they come up against the top teams, they've only won one in ten."

Humphrey asks Lescott "if Bielsa can improve the quality of a player, why does that leave a ceiling?" Lescott seems flummoxed by the anchorman's logic and irrelevantly refers to "Pep Guardiola and Sir Alex Ferguson, the two best managers to have graced the Premiership, they adapted their formations."

Humphrey remarks that no fewer than 163 players formerly coached by Bielsa have gone on to be coaches themselves, mostly successfully. Ferdinand leavens his doubts with some praise – "there's no denying this guy's a great coach"- but still wonders whether Leeds can survive at this level for more than one season. He concludes by focusing specifically on City versus Leeds "the only thing I look at as a player, when you're in the dressing room knowing you're not gonna adapt tactically to the best team in the land firing on all fronts and probably they're going to lose by a few goals and be exposed, how will they feel about that?"

What's not mentioned in this discussion is that on paper Leeds' task is not as formidable as it would have been say a couple of weeks earlier. City, whose defence has greatly improved since the two teams clashed six months earlier, are runaway leaders of the Premiership, virtually Champions-Elect although there's an outside chance of neighbours United catching them.

The thing is that City aren't at full strength –indeed nowhere near it. But this is due to Pep Guardiola's decision to prioritise the Champions League quarter-final second leg. Travelling to Dortmund a few days later, City's match is delicately poised with a narrow lead but having conceded an away goal to the Bundesliga side. Accordingly

Guardiola rests Kevin de Bruyne, Ilkay Gundogan, Mahrez, Walker, local boy and new England international Phil Foden and Portuguese centre back Ramon Dias who's become a vital component of their revitalised rearguard. In addition, the soon- to-depart veteran Sergio Aguero is injured.

These matters didn't come into the pundits' prognoses and it's almost as if they're convinced that whatever team Guardiola puts out, it will be too strong for Leeds.

Leeds too are not at full strength with Jack Harrison ineligible to play against his parent club and Rodrigo still struggling against an accumulation of injuries. In the circumstances Helder Costa replaces Harrison and Tyler Roberts continues instead of Rodrigo. Leeds are in their maroon third kit.

Marcelo Bielsa's strategy's clear from kick-off. It's to utilise Raphinha's ball skill –something as yet not experienced by City – to expose the undoubted weakness of Mendy and the probable rustiness of Nathan Ake who hasn't played since Boxing Day. Unfortunately Raphinha won't be at his best in this game, his prowess with corners and free kicks seeming to have deserted him. That said, his dribbling's a constant danger to the home side.

In the second half of the season Raheem Sterling's been super-seded by Phil Foden and, selected only intermittently, hasn't scored for almost two months.Yet this time he plays.

In the opening minutes Raphinha makes a fool of Ake with a nutmeg only to misplace his pass behind Bamford. Sterling's seeking to get Ferran Torres away and the young Spanish winger evades Alioski yet Mendy strays blatantly offside and makes a mess of his shot anyway.

Gabriel Jesus is being marked by Liam Cooper and, seemingly nervous of Cooper's strength, he clumsily tackles him and brings the pair of them to the ground in the process.

Ayling and Raphinha link up well in furtherance of the game plan, forcing a corner off Ake. But it's well cleared by

Fernandinho. City's Brazilian captain's a veteran only a few weeks short of his 36th birthday. But he draws on years of experience plus an acute football brain and he'll be the main threat to Leeds throughout the game. Far from being clapped out, Fernandinho's moving effortlessly past Tyler Roberts. This infuriates Marcelo Bielsa and he slaps himself on the knees in frustration. The English-speaking players on the Peacock bench shout instructions to Roberts and Bielsa emphasises the urgency by punching the palm of his hand.

Another intelligent player in a Sky Blue shirt is the Ukrainian Alexander Zinchenko. Zinchenko took his time to adjust to the Premiership but has come into his own this season. Usually appearing at left back, he's moved into midfield as a result of Guardiola's changes.

Portuguese right back Cancelo's looking to get Jesus through with a quick and incisive pass, his move's foiled by Diego Llorente even though the Spanish guy catches Jesus on the ankle in the process.

Free kick taken and Stones lobs a through ball yet Diego Llorente calmly concedes a corner. Leeds' pundit-proclaimed weakness in this area is nowhere in evidence-in fact it's solidly defended but when they try to break out they're foiled by Cancelo.

With a quarter of an hour gone, the balance of possession is what anyone would have predicted, 70% in favour of City. Possession is of course de rigeur for Pep "I want the ball!" Guardiola. But while the Sky Blues' painstaking serial passing is only constricting the play, it's Leeds who are opening it up.

Soon there's an excellent move from the Peacocks which City are desperately fortunate to survive. Meslier instigates it with an excellent long kick straight to Raphinha –back to Ayling – thence to Kalvin Phillips and Phillips sweeps the ball forward to Raphinha, Raphinha's inside Ake in a moment and he plays it through to Tyler Roberts. Patrick Bamford's anticipating as usual and Roberts squares a low bouncing cross. Stones just manages to get the side of his boot on the ball to divert the danger as Bamford can do no more than get the heel of his left foot on it. It had looked for one fine moment as if only a blinding save from Ederson could have stopped Leeds scoring. Talk about fine margins!

Raphinha's looking pumped up and, working hard as he always does, he slide tackles Sterling as adeptly as a seasoned defender would have done. Sterling doesn't like it and the moment he's deprived of the ball he treads on Raphinha's ankle as the Brazilian lies on the ground. Raphinha's pain threshold isn't all it might be and this is the only credible explanation why Andre Marriner has turned a blind eye to the incident.

Varying their usual pattern, City create danger with Fernandinho making a strong run before passing to Cancelo whose cross to the far post has menace written all over it. Yet Alioski's alive to the danger, he jumps up high and brings off a fine defensive header, Sterling manages to get on the ball but he balloons his shot high over.

What stands out about City is that John Stones is seeing a lot of the ball, now Stones is of course technically better than most English centre backs, that's true, but he's not ingenious enough, whatever Guardiola might have thought, to penetrate Leeds'underrated defence. Sterling's as quick and skilful as ever but his old weakness in shooting resurfaces today; doubtless eager to impress Southgate who's skulking in the empty stand in bulky overcoat, heavy cap and black mask- that's 'Raheem Sterling' of course -always referred to by commentators under his full monicker.

It's Fernandinho who's the brains of City and his excellent chip from centre circle to 6 yard box puts Jesus through with a great chance to score. Here's where Diego Llorente comes right into his own. Anticipating the danger perfectly, he rises like a vertical takeoff plane to head the ball out for a corner. When it's delivered, Leeds' defence is excellent. Torres, hesitating momentarily, tries a shot but finds it splendidly blocked by Liam Cooper who was shouldered to the ground in the goalmouth skirmish, the ball rebounds to Jesus but his shot's blocked by Bamford at the expense of another corner which is well and truly cleared.

City resume their incessant attacks and Zinchenko sprays a dangerous pass wide left to Jesus yet Llorente's quick to make up ground and put the ball into touch even as he falls. Without question Diego Llorente's making a decisive difference to Leeds' defence.

Halfway through the first half, a rare Leeds error. Meslier dawdles with the ball then misplaces his short pass to Llorente forcing the centre back into a hurried clearance whereupon Mendy pressurises Ayling into a mistake, the ball runs to Sterling, he sits down Ayling and shoots but this time Leeds' right back middles it and Dallas follows up to blast the ball clear. The City forwards are moaning for a penalty on the grounds that the ball went from Luke Ayling's chest to his elbow, had it been granted it would have been a very harsh decision but fortunately Mr Marriner brushes their appeal aside.

Zinchenko's to the fore again acting as Fernandinho's lieutenant, he aims a dangerous cross for Sterling which Llorente promptly heads clear. The man from Madrid always seems to have time at his command.

Stones and Fernandinho combine, the Brazilian veteran shoots and Meslier clears with his leg, Marcelo Bielsa, hitherto scrutinising calmly from his crouch, senses slackness and bawls his keeper out.

Ake's looking distinctly flustered and he's booked for bringing Bamford down as Leeds' centre forward was ghosting past him.

For all City's multiple passes, they're failing to create danger. In his technical zone Guardiola seems increasingly agitated; frowning incessantly above his grey- flecked beard, he suddenly looks a lot older than 50.

Yet City have an excellent chance to score, unsurprisingly created by Fernandinho, he makes a strong run, he's too smart for Roberts, he prompts Cancelo, Llorente's drawn out of position after Costa can't get a tackle in; Sterling's escaped from Llorente for the first time in the match, he's clear to shoot from the 18 yard line but he can only side foot it four yards wide.

Phillips is dispossessed by Bernardo only because the Portuguese got in a sly kick undetected against Kalvin's calf, Jesus goes off on a long run but Cooper thwarts his shot with a cracking block. Phillips complains to Mr Marriner about the foul not given but gets no change out of the Brummie ref.

41 minutes and Leeds break through, Helder Costa hears Bielsa's voice in his ear on the touchline and bucks himself up. "Move! Move!!"- he does as he's told and, tussling for the ball with Cancelo, he gets the benefit of a lucky rebound before slipping a good pass to Bamford.

Until this moment in the match Stuart Dallas has been jogging unobtrusively about mainly concerned about helping out in defence, now he senses something, he moves effortlessly beyond Fernandinho, him and Bamford are on the same wavelength and Patrick finds him with a lovely little pass. Stuart strikes the ball first time from the edge of the box perfectly aimed just wide of Ake against the base of the post whence it veers abruptly into the far corner with Ederson utterly defeated.

Dallases "yes!" is sufficient for the undemonstrative Ulsterman. Marcelo Bielsa clenches his fists in satisfaction.

Yet within two minutes all the good teamwork comes unstuck; Leeds are caught napping after a throw-in, Ayling fails to get on to Jesus who strides ahead, Jesus is Cooper's man of course and Liam sends the Brazilian crashing to the ground with a rugged challenge.

Marcelo Bielsa senses danger, leaping to his feet with an angry dismissive gesture indicating his frustration that Cooper has given

Mr Marriner a decision to make. Fortunately —or so it seems —he restricts himself to an instant yellow card. Yet soon David Coote, the controversial Coote, is in his ear from Stockley Park, VAR intervention is signalled on the massive scorescreen.

"I got the ball!" shouts Cooper —and indeed he did, hooking it high into touch. But Sky's replays depict a fearsome challenge with Cooper's bootstuds impacting the back of Jesuses' knee and the little Brazilian receiving extensive treatment. Even so, Cooper had kept his trailing foot grounded and Jesus has resumed with a grin, seeming undaunted after Leeds' skipper's allegedly ferocious tackle.

Skype call on their resident ref Peter Walton for his view and, initially, Walton states his belief that a yellow's sufficient. By this time, however, Andre Marriner's jogging to the monitor. He turns promptly away from it, ostentatiously places a yellow in his back pocket, brandishing a straight red instead. On the massive Etihad screen it indicates 'serious foul play.'

Dallas looks disbelieving, Llorente frowns in dismay, Cooper walks, muttering to Mr Marriner "I got the fuckin' ball!" and shaking his head. Peter Walton illogically concludes that Cooper has been slightly unlucky but it was a deserved dismissal just the same. Whatever, it's Leeds only red of the season.

At the touchline the departing skipper shakes hands with his replacement, Pascal Struijk. Obliged to sacrifice a player, Bielsa nominates Bamford.

Three minutes of the first half remain and first of all a free kick needs to be taken. Shocked Leeds' fans, their delight at having taken the lead dissipating like a burst balloon, hold their collective breath watching on TV all over the land and overseas as Zinchenko lines it up. He flights it cleverly yet the leaping John Stones can only get the back of his head on the ball and mercifully it flies a foot over.

The second half begins with Leeds keeping eight men behind the ball. The size of their task scarcely needs spelling out —fully 45

minutes to keep at bay a team noted for their expertise in possession. Yet Bielsa hasn't shut the door on the possibility of victory,
there are two outballs via Costa and Raphinha.

John Stones is revelling in the prospect of extra space, he
surges through midfield and wins a free kick. Phillips questions
the award –"hey ref, what's that for?" The Leeds lad's in combative
mood, the situation suits him. Zinchenko takes the kick but he can
find no breach in the wall.

Zinchenko thinks he spots an opening, he looks to send Jesus
through but Phillips blasts the ball clear hard and high.

Stones is striding about, looks like he thinks he can win this one
single-handed, he turns provider for Zinchenko who reckons he's
spotted a gap, he's wrong because Meslier dives on the ball. He's
well and truly got it within his grasp when Sterling follows up and
treads on his forearm. Meslier jumps up at once without complaint
yet Mr Marriner should have stepped in and booked the offender –
probably he thinks it's a matter of momentum but unquestionably
Sterling could have pulled up and certainly should have done.

56 minutes and Guardiola has seen enough, the team he sent
out haven't got the guile to penetrate Leeds' defence so on in place
of Ake comes Ilkay Gundogan, the team's top scorer with a goal
every other game. The black- bearded German with his face set
like flint, he'd hoped to sit this one out now it's down to him to
energise his jaded teammates. And whaddya know, there's Kevin
de Bruyne pacing around. It looks like he's about to make an
entrance but Guardiola changes his mind and sends the Belgian
big star back.

Stones shoots, it rebounds off Gundogan and goes behind yet,
when Bernardo Silva appeals for a corner, Mr Marriner agrees.
From the corner Cancelo tries a snapshot, the ball loops up and
Pascal Struijk heads it powerfully away from danger.

Soon an hour has gone by and Leeds are holding out; Llorente
marshals the defence, this is the selfsame guy who seven games

ago had been written off as a busted flush, now he appears in his true colours, the man Bielsa and Orta were determined to sign, not merely a Spanish international but a truly world-class central defender.

Alongside Llorente: Pascal Struik's a towering presence, physically rugged and dominant in the air; Kalvin Phillips is up for the scrap, no City boy gonna get the better of a lad from Leeds; Stuart Dallas' brains and lungs, the most underrated player in the Premiership, if he was English the pundits would be barking at Southgate to bring him into the fold but, where Stuart comes from, surrender is never an option; Gjanni Alioski the last thing he can be accused of is lack of endeavour-what's more he's walking tall after North Macedonia's defeat of Germany; Luke Ayling acting skipper shouting the odds and pointing the gaps that need plugging; Tyler Roberts working his socks off, same as he always does.

The question has to be asked –but the pundits will never ask it – is character, individual and collective, coming into the equation? And who has more of it –the squad assembled at colossal expense on Abu Dhabi liquid gold or the lads from Leeds brought together unheralded in Championship days?

Behind the defensive wall is Illan Meslier, maturing minute by minute in the heat of battle, coming out of his goal to head off attacks, he's a real sweeper-keeper now, his lime green jersey's everywhere.

All the while Marcelo Bielsa has been pondering, it's not that he's abandoned all thought of counter-attack but the defence, stalwart as it is, needs an extra boost. The time was when he had three of his four central defenders crocked, now, though one's been sent packing by the ref, the others are all healthy, so, on 63 minutes he brings on Robin Koch. Recently Koch's been limited to a few minutes here and there coming off the subs' bench, not to be wondered at for a guy completing his recovery from a torn meniscus.

Now Koch has less than half an hour to hold out and, if he does nothing else, he'll be an extra body in the defensive wall.

Alioski mistimes his tackle on Torres and is booked. He snaps at the ref in Albanian, very useful to let off steam in a language no one else understands! From the freekick Gundogan tries a snap-shot, it's blocked, the rebound falls to him and he lets fly with a fierce left foot half volley, it's good to see it going high and wide.

Guardiola looking increasingly agitated, he'd staked a bundle on Stones but now the burly boy from Penistone's being marked by Struijk and he's getting no change out of the man from Amsterdam.

City are being reduced to long range strikes, Zinchenko hits one and Phillips heads it out, Cancelo hits another and Meslier grabs it, no bother. Crosses are not usually part of City's armoury but Torres tries one now and Phillips brusquely kicks it clear.

Gundogan tries to pull a fast one but he's outguessed by his compatriot, Koch. Then, when Phillips pushes ahead to start a break, he's cynically brought down by Stones. Mr Marriner fails to intervene and Kalvin, after flinging up his arms in outrage, jumps to his feet and dashes back into the fray.

As soon as Llorente's calmly cleared the danger Phillips vents his exasperation with the man in yellow, snarling "fuck off!" Then he catches himself on about the possibility of punishment and mutters more remarks under his breath. Mr Marriner must have heard his initial outburst but he's been turning a blind eye for 70 minutes and now he opts to turn a deaf ear.

Fernandinho unleashes a 30 yard piledriver yet Meslier brings off a steel -wristed parry.

73 and Guardiola plays his penultimate card, removing Mendy and sending on Phil Foden; save only for Kevin de Bruyne he's been forced to field his full attacking cohort.

76 1-1 after half an hour's incessant effort, City finally get their equaliser not due to any lapse in the Leeds defence but through working a much faster passing sequence between Fernandinho,

Bernardo and Torres and it's the 21-year-old ex-Valencia man who nets. Meslier was unlucky to lose his footing for a moment just before the successful strike.

Diego Llorente rallies the troops with an immediate shout of "come on!"

In the closing minutes City keep pressing forward and Sterling, quiescent for much of this half, sets off on a long run yet Koch is spot on when it comes to tracking back and he halts the little Neasden geezer in the D.

Llorente finally triggers a counter, sending Raphinha away on a run only to be cynically tripped by Bernardo Silva who's booked.

Five minutes left and Leeds look bound to score, a splendid 25 yard pass from Phillips sends Raphinha racing through with only the keeper to beat, this is the moment every Leeds fan's been hoping for yet Raphinha's kept at bay by a perfectly executed tackle from Ederson. Guardiola has always maintained that Ederson's good enough to play as an outfielder for many a good club side and this seems to prove the point; Raphinha, stunned to be thwarted in this fashion, later chuckles briefly at the insouciance of his compatriot.

Three minutes of stoppage time, surely Leeds will hold out yet within seconds they do far more than that; Meslier, alert as ever, spots an outball possibility; obsessed with Raphinha, City have forgotten about Costa on the opposite wing, Meslier finds him with a really good pass, Costa transfers briskly to Alioski, Stuart Dallas, looking like a man who's taken an oxygen hit, runs ahead-if only Alioski can find him; Alioski's pass looks inelegant, more of a kick truth to tell but it's wonderfully accurate and Dallas latches on to it, holds off Stones' desperate challenge and confronts Ederson. Ederson, said by some goalkeeping experts to have usurped his fellow countryman Alisson as the world's finest yet he comes out to the challenge with his feet carelessly spread.

That's it, Stuart Dallas pulls off a nutmeg strike, rolling the ball into an empty net. What a helluva goal, a mix of energy, vision and composure! Dallas runs to the corner flag and, in his exuberance, pushes it down. All smiles, he calls to his teammates to join him and they do with Gjanni Alioski jumping for joy after his own crucial contribution.

As for the crew in blue, Stones picks up the ball from the back of the net and boots it angrily upfield while Ederson spits out. Pep Guardiola, fawned on for years by the media as an incomparable coach and now touted to win the quadruple, hurls his water bottle down twice in rage while de Bruyne, the man he didn't dare risk, stands on the sidelines in his orange bib glaring in disdain at the scene.

Marcelo Bielsa knows full well there's almost three minutes remaining, no way must this lead be surrendered and the best way of doing that is to attack an already stunned City.

Fernandinho looks to start a City counter but he misplaces his pass sending it right to the feet of Raphinha of all people, Raphinha sprints ahead yet Fernandinho disgraces himself with a violent bodycheck, hurling Raphinha to the ground.

Mr Marriner has no option but to act. He promptly produces yellow but undoubtedly he should have sent Fernandinho off. The City captain did not get the ball, scarcely seeming to even try. His spiteful foul was far worse that Liam Cooper's and he should have been made to pay the full penalty.

Fernandinho's transgression's almost the last act of this momentous match. All that's left is the brief appearance of Jamie Shackleton as Raphinha has to be helped off.

After the final whistle, Guardiola has composed himself to place a congratulatory arm round the shoulder of his old mentor Marcelo Bielsa. As for Bielsa, he smiles warmly in satisfaction.

Leeds have been utterly vindicated by the turn of events. Had their victory been achieved by all eleven men, pundits would have been quick to point out that it had been only at the expense of what they would've called Guardiola's 'second string.' Yet, as it was, Cooper's dismissal had precluded that interpretation. Instead of the usual claptrap about Bielsa having "no Plan B", here, limited to ten men, he had not only held out against the possession-based Premiership leaders, but had actually inflicted defeat on them.

In his postmatch interview Marcelo Bielsa characteristically showed no hint of triumphalism. Referring to the disparity between City's total of 29 shots and one goal as against Leeds two successful shots on target, he permitted himself a brief moment of amusement at the beautiful absurdity of football. Yet he left no doubt that Leeds had fully deserved to win.

Back in the BT Sport studio once the match was over, Jake Humphrey, exclaiming "what a game of football!", invited the pundits to comment. Rio Ferdinand said "yes, Bielsa was forced to adapt when they went down to ten men –they adapted and they were magnificent and fully deserved their victory today"

Seeming to sense that Joleon Lescott remained unconvinced, Humphrey pointed at him, saying "listen! going down to ten men forced him to play the way he did but it didn't force him to go looking for the winner in added on time at the end. That was brilliant!"

Looking uneasy, Lescott conceded–"yeah, amazing." But, searching for an explanation for a turn of events he hadn't remotely anticipated, he could only say "it forced them to make a tweak to their setup." The way he saw it "City had so many players so high, it always gives you an incentive to push men forward and this is what they did." What's more, Lescott was quick to pin blame for the winning goal on City's centre back. "John Stones'll be disappointed –he put a lot of energy into running high up the pitch but it reduced the amount of energy he had to make that saving run."

Seeming to think it was pointless to contradict Lescott, Humphrey cut to a BT Sport colleague interviewing Stuart Dallas. Stuart said "we showed a different side of ourselves today. We obviously had to change when we went down to ten men. We're normally man for man but, when you lose a player, you've got to play between two opponents."

The interviewer persisted —"that's the thing about Leeds, they never give up" only for a frowning Dallas to retort "you must never give up no matter who you play for!"

BT Sport's coverage of Manchester City versus Leeds, detailed as it was, revealed exactly the same misapprehensions as shown in their treatment of previous matches and mirrored Sky's coverage of Leeds. Ferdinand and Lescott were following in the footsteps of other pundits in focusing on heavy defeats suffered by Leeds against Leicester, Palace, United and Spurs in the first half of the season. But in the second half, with the sole exception of the Whites' defeat at the Emirates, there was no equivalent. In the first half Leeds were conceding almost two goals per game. Yet in the second half (with seven games remaining) their rate of concession was barely more than one per game.

Clearly pundits on both main football channels attributed Leeds' early heavy defeats to Bielsa's adventurous style. With the sole exception of the astute Jermaine Beckford, they failed to point out that Leeds often had three central defenders missing through injury; Cooper intermittently but the newly recruited Diego Llorente and Robin Koch out long term. Once a regular central defensive partnership had been established, the flow of goals against them had been stemmed.

While Rio Ferdinand had rightly praised Leeds' levels of concentration and reserves of energy after being reduced to ten men, it was left to Stuart Dallas to have the final word in the discussion just as he had the winning shot in the match. While Stuart didn't comment explicitly on the issue of character, something which no pundit dared to bring up, his stunning retort "you must never give up no matter who you play for" touched the heart of the matter.

CHAPTER 7

SPURS CRUSHED

As Spurs waited at windswept Elland Road for midday kick-off on May 8, they clung to the fading hope that, standing only seventh in the Premiership table, they might still achieve a final flourish and finish in a Champions League place.

Much had changed with Tottenham Hotspur since the reverse fixture which they won four months earlier. Above all the dreaded José Mourinho was gone. The apostle of defence and public critic of his own team had been fired by billionaire boss Daniel Levy. Whilst pondering possible candidates for the Portuguese coach's successor, Levy had appointed 29-year-old Ryan Mason as interim manager.

Regardless of Mason's inexperience, Spurs presented a genuine threat. They had their two great strikers, the sleepy-eyed assassin Harry Kane and the gleeful goal grabber Son Yeung Min. What's more, Dele Alli, shut out by Mourinho due to his perceived reluctance to track back, had been recalled. Sporting a new hairstyle replete with Ellis band, he looked different and his innate skill made him potentially dangerous. The final man in an adventurous four- pronged attack was Gareth Bale, on loan from Real Madrid, disdained by Mourinho for alleged laziness, yet widely considered a world-class player till only a year ago. What's more, Spurs were captained by the great French goalkeeper, Hugo Lloris, a World Cup winner in 2018.

BT Sport pundits focused almost wholly on Spurs in the buildup and were reminiscing fondly about how, two years to the day earlier, the Londoners had beaten Ajax in the CL semi-final with the last kick of the game. That was when the Brazilian Lucas Moura, now on the Spurs bench, had scored a second half hat-trick. And, whaddya know, Tottenham were in the same elegant dark green shirts they'd worn in the Johan Cruyff Arena.

Belatedly turning to Leeds, BT then announced the team news. Of the Whites' injured players, Helder Costa was out for the rest of the season but Kalvin Phillips, Raphinha and Rodrigo were all on the bench. Marcelo Bielsa hadn't selected Ian Poveda but had given Stuart Dallas the opportunity to demonstrate his extraordinary versatility on the right wing. Robin Koch would deputise for Phillips in defensive midfield with Klich and Roberts further forward. Liam Cooper, his three-game suspension completed, had picked up a knock in training and the central defensive partnership would continue to be Llorente and Struijk.

One thing the two teams had in common was the hybrid pitch which Tottenham had sold to Leeds earlier in the season. Once the subject of severe criticism, it was now said to be holding up remarkably well. Though it had been pissing down in Leeds since dawn, the groundstaff had been working their socks off to get it in good shape.

From the word go Gareth Bale was hugging the right touchline so tight that the commentators speculated that Ryan Mason expected him to make hay at the expense of Alioski who'd had a nightmare at Brighton. It was soon clear, however, that Alioski was well and truly pumped up for this match and would produce a fine attacking display.

Diego Llorente and Pascal Struijk were clearly facing the sternest test yet of both their individual ability and their partnership.

Leeds begin well but, in the fifth minute, Kane serves up a crafty chip beyond Struijk looking for Son. Llorente clears the danger at the expense of a corner. The flag kick produces a training ground manoeuvre with Kane flicking the ball low off his studs into the heart of the goalmouth. Robin Koch confidently clears.

Shortly afterwards Leeds exploit a mishit crossfield ball by Spurs' Spanish left back Reguilon. Seeking to find Bale, the Spaniard's weak effort's intercepted by Alioski who clips a pass to Harrison, Harrison finds Bamford with a brilliant reverse pass then Bamford swerves away from the dour Belgian Alderweireld before cracking a low angled shot which forces Lloris into a fine save plunging to his left to turn the ball behind his far post.

Two successive corners follow, from one of which Struijk has a solid chance but he volleys over the bar, covering his face in vexation at a missed opportunity. At the other end Leeds' defence looks solid and commentator Steve McManaman's rasping Scouse voice is heard insisting that "Leeds used to be gung ho at the start of the season but they've had to adapt." Clearly McManaman has not grasped how badly Leeds were weakened by the serious injuries to their two newly signed central defenders.

In the 10th minute there's an almost comic episode resulting from blatant shamming by Spurs' controversial Ivorian right back Serge Aurier. After Harrison beats him all ends up, Aurier glares at Klich before belatedly deciding to fling himself down clutching his face. His pathetic dissimulation cuts no ice with purple-shirted referee Michael Oliver who would have been well within his rights to have booked the offender.

It's good to see Klich playing with real vigour once again, something quickly noted by Spurs' rugged Danish midfielder Hojberg who grabs the Pole by the neck as he's speeding past him. Once again a booking would have been in order.

After 13 minutes Leeds take a thoroughly deserved lead with a splendidly worked goal. Luke Ayling's long crossfield ball's touched on first time by Dallas to Roberts who beats Reguilon and passes back to the advancing Koch, Koch quickly spots Jack Harrison well clear of the slack-marking Aurier and promptly feeds him, Harrison skips past Aurier and whips a deadly dropping cross through the goalmouth, Eric Dier the grim- faced, close-cropped Cheltenham chap seems unnerved by Bamford's presence and unwisely leaves it to Reguilon to clear the danger, Reguilon makes a complete mess of it and would have scored an own goal had it not been for Lloris' desperate dive. The Spurs captain manages to flip the ball away but his effort's in vain-Stuart Dallas pounces on the ball as it flies off the wet turf and lashes it into the roof of the net.

Marcelo Bielsa rejoices calmly in the goal, sipping his coffee imperturbably even as he quietly clenches his left fist. He had of course identified the wayward Aurier as a weak link and had tasked Alioski and Harrison with exploiting his vulnerability at every opportunity.

Spurs look to hit back and their underrated Argentinian mid-fielder Giovanni Lo Celso prompts Dele Alli with a good pass, he in turn finds Son who shoots powerfully only for Koch to bring off a fine block.

Leeds are moving really well but Marcelo Bielsa's quick to rebuke Tyler Roberts for playing the ball when he was in an offside position.

Against the run of play, in the 24th minute, Spurs equalise with a brilliantly improvised goal.

Dele Alli beats Llorente and slides a clever pass for Son who's running in unmarked on the right at exactly the same time that Kane's decoy run takes Struijk with him. Dele Alli deftly plants a pass beyond Ayling by which time Alioski has reacted too slowly to Son's run and the South Korean coolly flicks his shot beyond a stranded Meslier.

Alioski stands with his arms extended downwards giving Llorente a reproachful look, he's about to say something until silenced by a shout from Bielsa, he wants no arguing between his players at any time.

A potentially dangerous Leeds move fizzles out after Koch's strong challenge robs Son, Koch passes to Dallas who feeds the unmarked Roberts but, just as Bamford makes a clever anticipating run between the central defenders, Roberts dithers before under-hitting a pass- the ball glances off Dier's feet and Spurs regain possession; Marcelo Bielsa's furious, jumping to his feet to call Roberts out before pacing away still muttering in exasperation.

Leeds target Aurier once again, Alioski starts the move with a pass to Klich who plays in Harrison, Jack makes short work of getting past Aurier, he changes feet in an instant and uses his right to deliver a fiery shot, it seems goalbound all the way yet Lloris executes a tremendous leap and uses his fingertips to prod it over the bar. Then he punches the corner ball deep away. Dapper and bemoustached, the great French keeper, son of a Monte Carlo banker, looks determined to thwart Leeds' brilliant lads.

Leeds are playing with terrific verve, their standouts are Harrison back to his brilliant best and Koch having by far his finest game in a white shirt but basically it's a collective effort, Spurs goal's under siege and when Koch delivers a ferocious 25 yard drive it's only a lucky deflection off Hojberg which keeps out the shot, nowt doin' from the corner and Spurs can breathe a sigh of relief –for the moment.

Yet totally against the run of play, right on the half hour mark, Spurs once again execute a quickfire gambit and get the ball in Meslier's net. It begins when Harrison's robbed by Lo Celso who wastes no time before feeding Son, Son finds Dele Alli at once and the man from Milton Keynes takes out Struijk and Llorente with a perfectly incisive pass which Harry Kane finishes with great aplomb, dinking the ball first bounce over Meslier.

At this point Leeds are grateful for a linesman's immediately raised flag. Neither Kane himself nor Dele Alli nor anyone else in a green shirt protests the decision. Yet, when it's referred to VAR, Kane's only ruled offside by a hair's breadth.

The match has turned into a tremendous clash with two conflicting styles —Leeds swinging the ball about with fantastic inter-passing while Spurs respond with quickfire vertical moves dependent on their quick -thinking deadly finishers.

Undoubtedly Aurier's Spurs' weak link, out of his depth against Leeds' pace and penetration. He trundles about all baleful glare and daft protuberant beard but he has the devil's own luck as he somehow escapes putting through his own net; Leeds' great move begins with a series of passes involving Ayling and Koch who slips a fine pass inside Hojberg to Klich, the Pole eliminates Reguilon with a cross to find Dallas dashing in wide right and it's Stuart's immediate tantalising cross out of Lloris' reach which bamboozles Aurier. Flinging himself into the air like a scalded cat, the Ivorian finds the ball hitting him on the back of his right calf before it bounces to safety off his left thigh-Leeds' move deserves to culminate in a goal but all they have to show for it is a corner from which nothing comes.

Two minutes later Leeds force the pace again with Koch's fine pass to Harrison, he surges contemptuously past Aurier and crosses to Dallas on the opposite wing, thence Dallas to Ayling before Dallas and Ayling swap quick short passes. Reguilon's run ragged into the middle of next week, indeed the whole Spurs' defence are at their wit's end trying to keep the Whites out, Leeds' linkup play's so natural it seems they could almost find each other in their sleep.

Eight minutes left in the first half and Mr Oliver makes his first serious mistake after Alioski's through ball for Harrison, Harrison gets beyond Aurier who can only resort to impeding him before dropping to the deck as if Harrison was the culprit; Jack's all set to test Alderweireld with a low cross searching for Bamford but as he reaches the byline the Geordie whistler blows him up for a foul,

Harrison's rightly livid –"what for?" he shouts then, emphasising his point with a sweeping gesture, he calmly continues–"he cut right across me!"

The one Leeds player who's struggling is Tyler Roberts and, after Koch's fine pass plays in Harrison, the winger varies the focal point of the attack with a cross to the Welshman who fails to get it under control with his head. Leeds are in the ascendancy again and throughout the entire half Meslier hasn't had a save to make.

Four minutes from half-time and the Whites deservedly regain the lead, Klich plays a long ball looking for Bamford yet Dallas gets on it and beats Kane who tries to trip him. Dallas staggers and falls but not before he's laid the ball off to Roberts; Mr Oliver plays advantage and it's Roberts to Harrison with Alioski cunningly nipping behind the winger's back reaching the byline before the Spurs' rearguard have sussed his intentions, Harrison's on the same wavelength, he plays the Macedonian through and Alioski cuts the ball back short beyond Alderweireld's extended leg, Bamford's read the move the whole way through and he instantly taps in.

After a five-game drought Patrick Bamford's back on the scoresheet with his 15th goal of the season.

Spurs make a lively start to the second half and within four minutes have the ball in Meslier's net. It's disallowed for blatant offside against Kane. The buildup was slick involving dele Alli, Bale and Lo Celso yet Kane knew he was yards off even as he insolently celebrated slotting the ball past the Leeds' keeper.

Soon Koch's booked for clipping Son's ankles as the South Korean looked to set up a counter-attack.

Leeds have simply not got going again with Roberts shooting wastefully wide and a rare error from Struijk yielding possession to Hojberg who finds Lo Celso thence onto Son, he skips past Llorente's attempted sliding tackle but fortunately his fierce shot can only hit the side netting.

There's further sloppy play from Roberts failing to find Klich when he spotted an opening and gestured for the ball. Almost immediately afterwards Roberts blunders again misplacing a pass to Harrison with Bamford moving ahead in wait for the move unfolding.

In the 57th minute Marcelo Bielsa has seen enough and he hooks the hapless Tyler bringing Raphinha back to the fold at last. But he instructs the Brazilian and Harrison to swap wings. This is aimed at troubling Aurier even more. Mind you, Reguilon, now Harrison's immediate opponent is, though not at Aurier's level, already showing signs of severe discomfiture. The arrival of Raphinha means that Dallas can move centrally to partner Klich.

With these changes made, Leeds are back in full swing and their superior fitness begins to tell. With the hitherto incessant rain easing off, they adjust better to the pitch conditions than Spurs do.

Spurs are increasingly reliant on isolated bursts but, given the ability of their strikers, they remain dangerous. There's nifty inter-play between Kane and Son, Son shoots yet Struijk hurls himself into a block.

Reguilon's in big trouble against Raphinha. He can only resort to fouling the Brazilian and gets booked for his pains.

Struijk dispossesses Son with a truly tremendous tackle, per-fectly timed and with all his muscular power behind it. It brings roars of approval from the Peacock bench.

Leeds surge forward majestically: Koch –Dallas –a crossfield ball for Harrison, Reguilon's so perplexed he can't even manage to foul the Leeds' winger –a pass to Klich and the bearded Pole, enjoying his best game for months, fires a swirling shot only for Lloris to pull off another fine save, the corner's cleared but only for a moment, Aurier fouls Raphinha, Dallas takes the freekick but puts it over the bar.

66 minutes and Ryan Mason realises he must do something to try and stem the flow. He removes dele Alli who's faded and

Gareth Bale who never got started. On come Lucas Moura and the volatile Argentinian Lamela. Scarcely is the baldheaded Brazilian on the pitch than he's booked for shoving a forearm into Alioski's face.

Now comes something clean out of the blue in the context of this match, Serge Aurier of all people almost restores parity for Spurs. He barges past Raphinha and fires a fierce cross shot from the edge of the box. Meslier, rarely troubled hitherto, pulls off a truly great save, leaping at full stretch. Replays shows that it was even better than it looked at first sight since the ball took a marginal deflection off Alioski.

The Lo Celso corner brings further trouble to the Whites. It's headed clear yet Jack Harrison, in his eagerness to launch a counter, finds himself tussling with Reguilon just outside the box. Harrison's a tough lad in these sorts of situations but he forgets in the heat of the moment that he's right in front of the ref. He shoves Reguilon off the ball, the Spaniard makes a meal of it and Mr Oliver promptly whistles for a free kick.

Harry Kane relishes the prospect of a strike from just wide of the D. His venomous shot cannons off the top of the crossbar. Illan Meslier was just under the ball and might have got a saving glove on it if he felt he needed to.

Spurs are attacking recklessly. They can't afford to lose and their bench are in full cry yelling on "Arry and Sonny gerratem!" But it's Lamela who produces a strong low angled shot. Meslier improvises a save. Going down star-shaped he kicks the ball for a corner with his extended left leg. Robin Koch's so relieved he jabs fists with Meslier in congratulation. Nothing comes from the corner.

Marcelo Bielsa, sensing tension in the White ranks, decides to take off Bamford with 12 minutes remaining and send on Rodrigo. Mason does his best to reply by summoning Ndombele.

Eight minutes remaining, Leeds must hold out and look to clinch it with a third goal. Koch, at the peak of his game, dispatches a fine pass to Rodrigo in the centre circle. Rodrigo and Harrison swap passes before bringing in Klich. Klich smites a fine shot, it's over Lloris but sadly it's over the bar as well, Mat grits his teeth in dismay.

Lucas Moura sets off on a long run almost as if he thinks he can dribble his way through the entire Leeds' defence. Pride before the fall and Alioski robs him. A distinctive figure as always, all blonded bonce and short fast strides, he surges up the flank and finds Klich, Klich to Koch, in free-flowing counter-attack, Spurs dishevelled, only one defender plus Lloris can possibly foil Leeds now, Koch –Raphinha rampant down the left flank –all the while Rodrigo's perfectly read the move and now he's right on hand for Raphinha's square pass, Rod fairly belts the ball home. It's his first goal for four months, his season racked with illness and injury, but he looks more relieved than exhilarated, pointing to his Brazilian buddy as the provider. Soon Koch joins them, leading other team-mates in a celebratory embrace.

It may be 3-1 with only six minutes left on the clock but Marcelo Bielsa quickly cuts short the celebrations. Looking to disturb Spurs' rhythm with a substitution, he takes off Klich and on strides Kalvin Phillips eager to join the action.

Spurs have been crushed yet Bielsa wants another goal. In stoppage time it nearly comes, a fine move involving Struijk, Phillips and Alioski, Alioski crosses to the far post, Spurs manage to get it clear but Rodrigo gets on it and slips a clever pass to Dallas, Stuart's strong shot looks to put the icing on the cake but Hugo Lloris, Spurs' one real hero denies him.

In the post match interview Ryan Mason revealed his inexperience, complaining bitterly about Kane's first disallowed goal and claiming it was the turning point of the match. Far from it, in actual fact it was only Lloris' world-class saves which kept Spurs' margin of defeat within respectable limits.

Marcelo Bielsa expressed his delight with a Leeds' performance blending defensive solidity with attacking panache.

The result kept Leeds in ninth place in the Premiership table. More significant, however, was a detailed analysis the following day which indicated that, based on results in the second half of the season, the Whites would have finished fourth and on that basis qualified for the Champions League.

PART TWO

THE LADS: AN A-S OF THE LEEDS UNITED SQUAD

Alioski–Ayling–Bamford–Cooper–Costa-Dallas–Harrison– Hernandez–Klich-Koch-Llorente-Meslier-Phillips-Raphinha– Roberts-Rodrigo-Shackleton-Struijk

THEY CALLED HIM A NUTTER

EZGJAN ALIOSKI

During his seven years in Switzerland –at Young Boys Berne, Schaffhausen and Lugano – there were many serious minded supporters who questioned whether the little Macedonian of Albanian heritage was entirely sane. But Gjanni Alioski found a home from home when he arrived at Elland Road in 2017. He specialised in zany antics off the pitch and sometimes on it. Gurning, tongue lolling, rattling retractable tunnels, shoving his mug into TV cameras, muttering "I love Leeds, dirty Leeds" with a wicked grin, he threw himself into tackles with no half measures. He pitched in with goals right out of the blue and on one occasion dumbfounded an opponent by tackling him with his head at hip level. Leeds fans took him to their hearts and, among many similar tweets, the standout was "I love this fella, he's a fucking nutter."

Sports psychologists could point to Alioski as an extreme example of the dressing room joker and prankster ideal for dissipating tension pre-match, especially with worriers such as Jack Harrison. Then again there were those who wondered whether Alioski's irrepressible jocularity would survive in the era of Marcelo Bielsa.

But it did. Popular not only with fellow extroverts such as Kalvin Phillips and Luke Ayling but also with quiet man Pablo Hernandez, Alioski showed his value in cementing team spirit. Though there were times when, even as he carried out his defensive duties as diligently as he'd been told to, he was slow to react to developing danger. Equally, when going forward, he was prone to stray offside, a weakness which was jocularly commented on in an affectionate fan song about him.

Gjanni Alioski's most memorable match was at the Hawthorns against West Bromwich. He opened the scoring –forgetting about the home side's early own goal –by sprinting into the space opened up by the Baggies' naïveté and blasting a ferocious bullet of a shot which exploded against the inside of the far post and ricocheted into the back of the net. His celebration, exuberant even by his standards, consisted of a swallow dive where he buried his blond quiff into the flaking paint on the touchline. Was this what triggered his later nosebleed which ended up with his nostrils plugged with gauze? To cap it all, he was booked by Lee Mason for a high challenge even when Leeds were four nil up. The player he fouled was the smirking Diangana-had he been taking the piss before Alioski got even with him?

Alioski was the victim of deplorable social media abuse after the match with Arsenal where Nicholas Pepe was sent off for head-butting him. Defending him against allegations of provocation, Marcelo Bielsa noted that "Gjanni is a very passionate player, totally committed to the cause."

Whereas some thought his goal against West Bromwich was a one off, he came close to repeating it against Everton. In what looked like a carefully prepared training ground manoeuvre, he met an outswinging corner from Raphina with a ferocious left foot volley which cannoned off the post with Toffees' keeper Robin Olsen nowhere near it.

In the same game, however, he irritated his teammate Tyler Roberts by being 10 yards out of position. Admonished by Bielsa, he bizarrely took out his frustration by pushing down Everton's huge Colombian centre back Yerry Mina-who towered above him-and tapping him on the head as he fell. Alioski was substituted shortly afterwards.

Alioski had a nightmare against Arsenal at the Emirates. He was unable to cope with Bukayo Saka and was subbed off early in the second half.

It looked as if things might turn out the same way when Chelsea's Pulisic was roasting him at Elland Road but Alioski stuck to his guns and had the satisfaction of seeing the American substituted in the second half.

Returning to London, Alioski several times made a fool of himself at Craven Cottage. Scarcely had Fulham kicked off with a conventional long ball than Alioski decided to intervene though Struijk had it well covered. He only succeeded in heading it against Struijk whence it rebounded for Cavaleiro to dash in. Fortunately a prompt rescue act by Diego Llorente saved the day. Later Alioski perpetrated a ridiculously high back pass which Meslier fielded as Llorente kept the Fulham striker Maja at bay.

Fulham's approach was heavily physical and there was a clear danger Alioski would be drawn into retaliation first when he fouled the pugnacious Portuguese Cavaleiro and later when he grappled with Cavaleiro on the touchline. Fulham boss Scott Parker, doubtless scenting a yellow card and possibly a dismissal, bellowed "get yer arms down, you!"

But shortly afterwards there was a break in play when Stuart Dallas required extended treatment from the physios. Marcelo Bielsa took this as an ideal moment to have a word with Alioski. He was wise enough to know that hectoring the little Macedonian would be counter-productive so he patiently and calmly explained with restrained gestures. Alioski nodded respectfully to the head coach. Promising to behave himself, Gjanni was as good as his word thereafter.

Gjanni Alioski enjoyed himself no end in the ten man defeat of Manchester City. The situation was right up his street of course but, as well as defensive duties, he had probably his finest moment in a Leeds shirt when he planted a peach of a pass into Stuart Dallases' path for the winning goal.

Sadly Alioski had a nightmare against Brighton in the Amex Stadium. Targeted by wily manager Graham Potter he was attacked from the word go by the Seagulls' sprightly winger Leandro Trossard and roving centre forward Neal Maupay. In the 13th minute he was solely to blame for the opening goal, conceding a penalty by a clumsy challenge on Danny Welbeck which saw him slipping to the deck and grasping Welbeck's leg as he did so.

Later his defensive slackness let Trossard clean through and only the Belgian's wild shot prevented Brighton doubling their lead from another Alioski error.

Not for the first game Jack Harrison had to expend valuable energy bailing Alioski out and it was no surprise Marcelo Bielsa hooked him at half time.

Alioski's wildly fluctuating form manifested itself against Spurs. Expected by pundits to be severely troubled by Gareth Bale, he showed the lazy loanee scant respect. Not only that but he carried out Marcelo Bielsa's instructions to the letter, teaming up with Jack Harrison to humiliate Spurs' wild man right back Serge Aurier. True, he was somewhat at fault defensively when he reacted too slowly to Son's speedy run which led to Tottenham's equaliser. Called out by Bielsa for trying to shift the blame with a dodgy glance at Llorente, he got his act together at once.

Just before half-time he was a sight to behold as he craftily dodged behind Harrison's back and got to the byline before Spurs' defenders could blink. Promptly trapping Harrison's pass, he steered the ball back beyond Alderweireld for Bamford's tap in.

What's more, it was Alioski who began the move leading to the Whites' clinching third goal. Niftily dispossessing Lucas Moura, he proceeded up the left flank in his characteristic short fast stride pattern before playing Klich through.

Gjanni Alioski began what would be a memorable afternoon for him at Turf Moor with a shot so badly mishit it reached the corner flag and left him slumped with his head in his hands.

Midway through the second half he became embroiled in a confrontation with Burnley winger Dwight McNeil. When Alioski went down after McNeil's challenge, he found the winger stooping low over him clearly insinuating that the Macedonian had been shamming. Turning furiously to referee Graham Scott, Alioski asked "did you see that–what he done?" He appeared to be claiming that the Rochdale man spat in his face as he lay on the ground. For his own part, Alioski had clearly responded with a ludicrous gesture, tongue fully protruded, thumbs behind his ears and fingers waggling as he glared at McNeil.

Immediately afterwards Burnley manager Sean Dyche found it prudent to remove McNeil. Yet Mr Scott went over to the technical area and called the two managers towards him, revealing that McNeil had complained to the fourth official about Alioski's behaviour which, on the surface, seemed to be no more than the juvenile blowing of a raspberry.

No further action was taken against Gjanni Alioski and he survived to the last game of the season against West Bromwich sporting hair dyed as white as his shirt. His defensive lapses may have been embarrassing but he wore his heart on his sleeve in the cause of Leeds United.

A DIAMOND GEEZER

LUKE AYLING

The song was written ages before Luke Ayling was even born, as a matter of fact long before his uncle, England assistant manager Ray Lewington was born. It may even have been penned before Luke's grandad first saw the light of day. It's called 'The Lambeth Walk' after the London borough where the Aylings and the Lewingtons come from. It had seemed impossibly antwack until a couple of renditions of it were posted on YouTube in 2013 – since when they've had between them half a million views!

The song salutes the free and easy, confident, extrovert attitude said to prevail down Lambeth Way –"everything free and easy, do as you darn well pleasee!" And Luke Ayling's the absolute incarnation of the hundred per cent Cockney geezer. He started on Arsenal's books but they bluntly told him that, as they saw it, he wasn't up to scratch. Undaunted, he sought to make his way to the top the long way round, beginning at Yeovil Town in –as Luke called it –"sleepy Somerset."

After a spell with Bristol City, Ayling came to Leeds and it wasn't long before he was a big hit with the fans. Mind you, in his most celebrated moment Luke wasn't doing anything as laid-back as the Lambeth Walk. When he leaped into the air and volleyed a brilliant goal against Huddersfield Town he was so elated he tore off his headband and raced to his teammates with his shoulder length hair blowing in the wind. "Nice one, Bill!" they said, acclaiming him by his nickname.

As soon as Marcelo Bielsa arrived at Elland Road, Luke Ayling succinctly summed up the situation –"he's the greatest coach in the world so whatever he wants, we'll do it, yeah."

When Leeds regained their rightful place in the Premiership, Luke Ayling faced the devastating winger/striker Liverpool's Sadio Mane at Anfield in the opening game of the season. Within the first few minutes, he impudently nutmegged Mane, chuckled about it and took it in good part when the Reds' Senegalese ace got him one back in similar fashion shortly afterwards. He'd arrived in the big time and this was the proof of it.

Ayling had close to a nightmare against Newcastle at home when he was partially to blame for the Geordies' two set piece goals. For the first he failed to prevent Callum Wilson's flick-on which led to Hendricks scoring. His error for the second was worse-he scarcely got off the ground for Kieran Clark's header.

Adventurous as he was as a rampaging full-back, there was a very different side to Luke Ayling which revealed itself when he was called on to be a central defender. In this role against Manchester United–when he was vice captain into the bargain –he was dealing competently with Antony Martial only for Kalvin Phillips to dash over and offer unwanted assistance. In doing so Phillips left the man he was supposed to be marking, Bruno Fernandes, in the clear and, when the ball broke loose, Fernandes instantly slammed it into the net. The look on Ayling's face was cold enough to freeze beer!

Ayling was in the thick of things the day Leeds beat Leicester at the King Power Stadium. He was certainly at fault when the Foxes opened the scoring, having left a big gap between himself and Harvey Barnes, the scorer. But, far from hiding, Luke instigated the equalizer a couple of minutes later, intercepting an under-hit pass from Maddison and surging forward down the line with an imperturbable grin before finding Bamford who prompted Dallases' goal.

After a booking, he came to the ref's attention again shortly afterwards. Puzzled as to why, he grinned as Stuart Dallas told him his forehead was smeared with blood. Ordered to the touchline, he returned to the fray with his napper bandaged. Here was the essential diamond geezer, oblivious of temporary pain.

In interviews Luke Ayling remained his very down-to-earth self. He dismissed the notion that Leeds had become entertainers for the nation stressing instead how much fun it was for players to take part in all-out attacking football. That became even more marked with the emergence of Raphina as a potentially world-class winger in mid-season and Luke was right to give himself credit for the way in which he linked up with the Brazilian.

Ayling found himself floundering in the match against West Ham in the London Stadium. First of all he mistimed his tackle on Jesse Lingard sending the little loanee from Man U tumbling to the turf eyeballs popping and arms outstretched as he beseeched Mike Dean for a penalty. When it was duly granted, Luke protested vehemently, backed up by Diego Llorente who shouted "he got the ball!" From Llorente's point of view that's what it would have looked like and Luke himself had played to do just that. But replays showed that he'd caught Lingard's shin. The Hammers' Scouse left back Aaron Cresswell promptly had a word in his ear – 'forgerrit, la!'

But just as Luke had contrived to wipe out the memory of his error, he made another one when he reacted far too late to stop scrapper centre back Dawson, a man used to roughing it in the lower divisions, from charging in at a corner and heading the ball vigorously home.

Against Chelsea, however, Luke was in his element, skippering the side with Liam Cooper having been ruled out on grounds of illness. When Havertz looked certain to give the Blues an early lead, Ayling did enough to put the German off and his shot was saved by Meslier. He was involved in a bizarre incident when, with Chelsea pressing strongly, he tried to lash the ball clear only for it to strike Diego Llorente's chest, rebound over Meslier's head and roll back off the bar into the keeper's gloves. Luke grinned as he apologized to the Spaniard with a tap on the head.

Ayling was in the wars when he was flattened by an accidental elbow from Mason Mount. Hard as nails, Luke soon jumped up only to crock himself in a challenge he didn't need to make. Once again he bounced back swiftly.

When the recently booked Gjanni Alioski was blown up by ref Kevin Friend, Ayling feared the worst but, intervening on his teammates' behalf, he acknowledged the ref with a smile and a respectful nod as he pleaded for the little Macedonian's reprieve. It worked.

Shutting out the prolific Chelsea attack was a notable achievement and it was a measure of Leeds' newfound defensive zeal when Liam and Kalvin Phillips were seeing arguing over who let Chilwell in even though the Londoners' left back had fluffed his shot.

In the eighth minute of the clash with relegation battlers Fulham at Craven Cottage, Luke Ayling seemed to have scored a splendid goal only to have it scrubbed off at Stockley Park following Fulham's appeal which referee David Coote belatedly referred. Tyler Roberts had lofted a fine hanging cross beyond the far post where Ayling, racing in unmarked, made a huge leap and looped a header high above keeper Areola to drop perfectly into the far corner. Luke was understandably jubilant at his first Premiership goal and celebrated lustily in the style of a hair metal rocker. As his lengthy locks were loosened from his topknot, he beamed in delight, miming a guitar riff. While Fulham protested, Ayling's teammates embraced him. Even the normally serious-minded Diego Llorente was moved to mirth by Luke's uninhibited antics. Sadly his joy was cut short by the news from Stockley Park-the verdict was offside. "That can't be me, can it!" Luke expostulated. It wasn't of course but VAR had ruled Roberts the culprit. The picture showed the margin was ridiculously narrow.

Unfortunately Ayling was partly responsible for Fulham's undeserved equalizer shortly before half time. He was slow to react at a Cottagers' corner and beat the turf with self-vexation after the Dane Joachim Anderson stuck out a boot and the ball went in.

Later, Luke Ayling, determined to rise above Fulham's provocation, cracked a joke about it with Kalvin Phillips after Raphinha was cut down. The pair of them were on the opposite touchline swigging energy drinks, two resolute warriors above the fray. Fortunately Raphinha was soon fit to return to the action.

When Liverpool came to Elland Road, Luke Ayling was in his element. Revelling in the responsibility of captaincy –following Cooper's red card against Manchester City –he looked forward to an outing against Sadio Mane having got to grips with the dangerous Senegalese winger-striker in the reverse fixture. Since then Mane's form had declined and he was without a goal in nine games so it was no surprise when Ayling contained him well once again. True, Mane opened the scoring on the half hour but this was with a tap in after excellent play by Diogo Jota and Alexander-Arnold had outwitted Alioski and Meslier and Diego Llorente hadn't reacted quickly enough.

Luke's love of a laugh came to the fore after the out of form Firmino tripped him and was promptly booked by Anthony Taylor. Some had not welcomed Mr Taylor's appointment but in fact he had an excellent game showing complete impartiality and spot on decisions. A buoyant Luke played mind games with Andy Robertson straight afterwards, first staring him in the face then bursting into laughter. The stolid Scotsman was baffled, exclaiming "what's that for?" But Ayling was a master of gamesmanship and the often dangerous Robertson was put off his game.

Later in the match Ayling made his only mistake when he left the door wide open for Jota and had to be bailed out by Pascal Struijk. Luke showed his appreciation at once with a cheery pat on the shoulder for the big Dutchman.

Luke Ayling was in his element when he skippered the side for Manchester United's visit to Elland Road. His voice was ringing out confidently all over the shop. Leeds' massive defensive improvement in the second half of the season would, he knew, ensure no repetition of the Old Trafford scoreline. But Luke wanted to go one better than that and beat United. The only problem was referee Craig Pawson tending to give decisions in the Mancs' favour.

Ayling sussed the ref out early doors when he sturdily but fairly tackled Marcus Rashford. Rashford went down with a yelp and Mr Pawson gave a free kick. Luke was quick to protest but to no avail.

In the 20th minute Ayling was angry when a chipped ball from Harrison looking for Bamford struck Shaw on the elbow of his outstretched arm. He appealed instantly but Mr Pawson turned it down. Yes, it was referred to Mike Dean on VAR duties but, the way Luke saw it, the ref should have given the penalty in the first place.

If Marcus Rashford started out thinking he'd have an easy time of it against Ayling, he had another think coming when Leeds' skipper brought off a bloody good block from the Manc talisman's powerful shot.

Then came a remarkable incident when a long ball from Maguire found Rashford and Ayling competing for a 50-50 ball just outside the box. As Rashford sprawled to the turf, Mr Pawson raced up and booked Ayling even though it seemed obvious he'd lost his footing on a still slippery part of the notorious Elland Road pitch. "I just slipped!" protested Leeds' captain as he pointed to the spot, lying where he fell. Yes of course he'd knocked down Rashford as he slipped but that was a free kick and nothing more.

When he got to his feet, Luke was incensed. Striding towards the referee and jerking a thumb in the direction of the incident, he warned Mr Pawson– "you fuckin' wait for VAR before you book me!" he said, adding "that's not fuckin' fair!!" Then he pointed an accusing finger at the ref, staring at him full in the face as he emphasised "that's NOT FAIR!"

At this point Rob Hawthorne offered an apology to Sky viewers who "might have heard some inappropriate language." In actual fact while Luke Ayling did not speak as a politically correct person might've done, his reaction was that of an honest working man when faced with blatant injustice.

The incident spoke volumes about Leeds' historic grievance over being blamed when they were not in the wrong and, in contrast, the Mancs' sense of entitlement as media favourites that the balance of decisions should always be in their favour.

PROVING THE PUNDITS WRONG

PATRICK BAMFORD

The biggest taboo in British football may not be sexuality but class. And its most prominent victim has been Patrick Bamford. Throughout his career Bamford was undervalued by managers because of his posh background. Sean Dyche, the Burnley boss, was the most outspoken of these, bluntly accusing Bamford of "never having done a day's work in his life."

Had Patrick Bamford been a gifted cricketer or tennis player, his middle-class origins would've stood him in good stead. At his school, the feepaying Nottingham High School, they looked down on football and made him play rugby, where he shone as a fullback, demonstrating all his athletic ability and ballplaying intelligence.

But it wasn't rugby that Patrick wanted to play. Right from when he was a nipper, he loved football. So did his dad, Russell Bamford who, though he isn't the heir to the JCB family (which many people have wrongly supposed), is a wealthy company director in his own right. Russell's best friend was Nigel Doughty, the chairman of Notts Forest and it was there that the 17-year-old Patrick made his debut. Far from being treated with kid gloves, as Sean Dyche insisted, Bamford from day one was tasked with cleaning the bogs and scrubbing the dressing room floor.

In opting for a career as a professional footballer, Patrick was turning his back on a scholarship to Harvard, America's most prestigious university. His academic career had been outstanding, replete with star grades, and he spoke French and Spanish well. In addition he was musically gifted, a violinist, pianist and guitarist.

From Forest Bamford was signed by Chelsea but his career at Stamford Bridge was inglorious. Manager José Mourinho wanted tank strikers such as Didier Drogba not the likes of Bamford. Patrick went out on half a dozen successive loans. He was prolific with three clubs and goalless with another three.

Bamford glimpsed the big time with Middlesbrough but his career looked to have stalled. That was before Marcelo Bielsa arrived at Leeds and, a matter of weeks later, so did Patrick Bamford for a fee of £7 million.

Utterly uninterested in the niceties of the English class system, Bielsa judged a footballer on skill, intelligence and determination. He was quick to note Patrick Bamford's nimble even elegant movements and powers of anticipation and, when Bamford came back from a cruciate ligament injury months earlier than the medical staff had feared, his resolve.

There was however one time when Bamford disgraced himself and let his manager down badly. That was in the clash with Aston Villa in May 2019. Bamford hurled himself to the deck clutching his face despite never having been touched by Holland's El Ghazi, the man who was immediately red carded. Whilst Bielsa made no public statement on the incident, he made it unmistakably clear to Bamford that shamming was totally unacceptable.

Bielsa's tactical system was based on one lone striker and here the head coach had to choose between Bamford and the highly promising Eddie Nketiah, on loan from Arsenal. To the surprise of many fans, he opted for Bamford.

While only a minority, albeit vociferous on Twitter, angrily called out Bamford as a "posh cunt" for missing chances, many reasonable supporters genuinely doubted that he would ever make it in the Premiership. It wasn't that they disliked him, they just wondered if he was "too nice to play for Leeds." He was compared to his detriment with Lee Chapman, a clumsy mover intent on banging the ball into the back of the net. And image still seemed to be an issue. In contrast to most of his teammates with cheerful Wags by their side, Bamford's girlfriend was the unsmiling London model Michaela Ireland, prone to posting on Facebook about logical fallacies. Nevertheless thinking fans were content to rest their case on Bamford's total of 17 Championship goals which represented a ratio of better than one in three.

Patrick Bamford's moment of truth came in the first Premiership match of the season. It couldn't have been a more difficult fixture, away at Anfield to current champions Liverpool who'd won the title by 18 clear points the previous year. Bamford's goal wasn't spectacular –the ball entered the Reds' net on the second bounce –but it was psychologically crucial in convincing Bamford that he was indeed a Premiership striker. It laid the foundation for his 17 goal haul in the season.

Bamford's strike stemmed from two things, Stuart Dallases' wonderfully audacious long ball and Virgil van Dijk's indolent reaction resulting in a rebound off his shin into Bamford's path. Anticipating perfectly, Bamford confounded van Dijk and Alisson Becker with a panther's crouch. As they converged on him only inches apart he used the side of his foot to clip the ball beyond them.

Though van Dijk's arrogance had opened up a chance for Bamford, the Dutchman was quick to close the gap. The fact remained that Leeds' centre forward, with only one previous Premiership goal to his name, had outwitted not only the best centre back in the world but also the finest keeper. He saw his chance and he took it. After that he would never look back.

To be a complete all-round centre forward Bamford of course needed to score with his head as well as with his feet. This he did at Bramall Lane where, in the late stages of a keenly contested Yorkshire derby, he finished off Jack Harrison's cross to secure victory. Typically modest, he admitted on camera that the ball had actually come off his nose.

Patrick Bamford's moment of triumph came at Villa Park, the scene of his earlier fall from grace. With the absent Holte End baying for his blood on Twitter and constantly goaded by burly centre backs Mings and Konsa, he rose to the occasion in splendid style, scoring a hat-trick.

His first was an opportunist strike following excellent build up play especially by Rodrigo. Yet it was more difficult than it looked. After Martinez' parry, Mings might still have got a block in or the keeper might have pounced on it but instead of hitting the ball in the same direction as he was moving, Bamford swerved and, even as he staggered, jabbed a shot into the near corner.

His second goal was astonishingly abrupt. Standing in the D with the Villa defenders waiting menacingly in front of him, he used minimal backlift to fire an absolute arrow of a shot swerving beyond the stunned Martinez' grasp.

Just as Bamford's second goal was better than his first, his third was even better than his second. He danced his way through a knot of Villans in the box as if they were statues before changing his body shape to lever his shot into the top corner.

This was a wonderful goalscoring trilogy highlighting Bamford's spatial perception, his agility and his speed of thought.

In the third minute at Stamford Bridge the tiny but nastily noisy Chelsea crowd were stunned to silence by a devastating Leeds goal on the counter-attack. The fulcrum of it was a fantastic 20 yard pass from Kalvin Phillips delivered from the junction of touchline and half way line and aimed for Patrick Bamford. Side spin sent the ball curving in beyond the burly centre back Zouma straight into Bamford's path. Keeper Mendy had committed himself outside the box ready to bring Bamford down if he had to. Yet Bamford evaded him with a balletic sidestep. Staggering for a second from his momentum, Patrick regained his balance and coolly sent the ball rolling into the empty net. True, Leeds went on to lose the game 3-1 but once again Bamford had registered a brilliant strike against top-class opposition and, not least, had shown his understanding with Kalvin Phillips.

When Burnley came to Elland Road just after Christmas Bamford came face-to-face with his old hostile manager Sean Dyche. In the third minute Leeds took Burnley by surprise with a long high through pass from Ayling to Bamford. Patrick cleverly got between the two vaunted centre backs Mee and Tarkowsky. Keeper Pope came lunging out and, just as Bamford neatly started to evade him, he sent Leeds' centre forward crashing to the ground. Referee Jones pointed unhesitatingly to the spot.

Had Pope not fouled him, Bamford would almost certainly have scored and now he took the penalty kick. Unshaven and looking menacing, his penalty was perfection. He sent Pope the wrong way and fired a ferocious but controlled shot high into the top corner. No keeper on earth could have prayed to save it. Bamford refrained from overt celebration, happy to receive the plaudits of his teammates. It was his 10th goal of the season, a perfect answer to his former manager, an unspoken "take that, Sean Dyche! Take that!!"

It wasn't only against Burnley that Pat Bamford showed signs of righteous anger. At Selhurst Park, against Crystal Palace, he had what was a perfectly good equaliser scrubbed off by VAR basically because his left hand was deemed to have placed him offside.

Undaunted, he scored again within a matter of minutes, ruthlessly finishing off a good move which began with a fine cross from Ayling and was continued by Klich's vigorous header. With the ball bouncing awkwardly, Bamford coolly chested it down before cracking a left foot half volley beyond the keeper. In the post match interview he was bluntly outspoken about VAR, not hesitating to startle the conformist pundits with his views. "It's daft!" he said before concluding "it's ruining the game!!"

After his Burnley penalty, Bamford experienced a four match drought, drawing blanks at the Hawthorns, the Tottenham Hotspur Stadium and St James Park and failing to score at home against Brighton. Mostly it was a case of missing chances albeit otherwise playing well but against Newcastle he could scarcely do a thing right and was subbed off in favour of Tyler Roberts.

Happily his class reasserted itself in the away victory against Leicester where he scored a brilliant goal after being perfectly prompted by Raphina. Swerving imperiously away from the rugged Turkish centre back Soyuncu, he found himself 8 yards wide and with the great goalkeeper Kasper Schmeichel facing him. But he timed his angled shot perfectly to see it fly over Schmeichel's head and nestle high in the far corner. In terms of sheer power of shot, this was his outstanding strike of the season.

He also had two assists. The first was a delicate pinpoint pass for Stuart Dallas to equalise. The second came in a Leeds counter-attack which saw him run from his own half to the box with only Schmeichel standing between him and the goal. But when Jonny Evans finally caught up with him, Patrick unselfishly square passed leaving Jack Harrison with a tap in. In the post match interview Marcelo Bielsa praised him saying it was typical of a player who put his team before himself. As different from Billy Bremner as chalk from cheese, Bamford had effectively resurrected the immortal Billy's wonderful motto!

At home against Crystal Palace, Patrick Bamford had the satisfaction of scoring his 100th career goal, achieved against the very club which, in the era of Alan Pardew, had ridiculously rejected him. Anticipating the development of a move involving Phillips and Klich, he made up ground from a deep lying position and was perfectly placed to clip home the rebound from Raphina's parried shot.

At the Emirates, although Bamford was relatively subdued for much of the game, he was harshly deprived of a penalty. Having instigated a brilliant quickfire passing sequence involving Roberts, Raphina and Shackleton, he burst through clear on goal only to be heavily sandwiched between Cedric and Gabriel and brought to ground. Cedric ostentatiously snarled at him as he fell and this may have deceived Stuart Atwell. Sky's Graeme Souness and Jimmy Hasselbaink plus Ian Wright on MOTD were unanimous that he'd been blatantly fouled in the box.

The following Friday at the Molineux Stadium Bamford saw his devastating strike scrubbed out by a ridiculous hair's breadth decision according to which his knee was deemed to have been centimetres ahead of Wolves centre back Coady's bootheel. It was reminiscent of what had happened at Selhurst Park but this time there would be no postmatch interview – doubtless because of media fear that Leeds' highly articulate centre forward would ridicule an innovation which he saw as ruining the game.

Patrick Bamford was back on the scoresheet against Southampton where he finished a rapid counter-attack begun by Llorente and continued with an excellent pass from Tyler Roberts to the centre forward. Bamford left Bednarek in his wake and deliberately hesitated, disconcerting Vestergaard before showing ice-cold aplomb as he steered the ball between the big Dane's shins and just wide of Alex McCarthy. That same quality of sangfroid showed up again, this time in defence, when he earned Meslier's thanks by calmly punting a dangerous ball high over the bar.

Bamford had an unhappy evening at the London Stadium during Leeds' two nil defeat to West Ham. Things had seemed to start all right with his accomplished finish to a cutback from Raphinha, but the goal was correctly disallowed due to the whole of the ball having gone over the byline a moment before the winger's cross.

Shortly after the interval, Bamford had an excellent opportunity to reduce the deficit when he received a wonderful slide rule pass from Diego Llorente, stabbed all of 25 yards and perfectly bisecting Dawson and Diop. But even as he clipped his left-footed shot wide of Fabianski, his radar was off kilter and the ball finished a yard and a half wide.

Worse was to follow in the 77th minute when, after a brilliant bout of interpassing, Raphinha rolled the ball to his feet as he stood just outside the six yard box. Using his weaker right foot, Bamford somehow managed to sky his shot high over the bar. He promptly flopped on his back in dismay at his gross blunder –only to be promptly called out by Marcelo Bielsa who wanted no such self -indulgence. Leeds' centre forward was to get to his feet at once and get on with the business.

Forced to limp off early against his old club Chelsea with a knock to the hip, Bamford made a speedy recovery and returned against Fulham. In the meantime he'd been snubbed by the stubborn Southgate who excluded him from the England squad despite having scored more goals than any Englishman other than Kane.

In the second minute at Craven Cottage, Diego Llorente delivered an excellent long ball, fully 35 yards bouncing into Bamford's path. Bamford's marker, the stocky Dane Joachim Anderson was quickly embarrassed, holding on to Bamford for dear life as they moved across the 18 yard line. At this point Bamford unselfishly heeded a call from the unmarked Tyler Roberts. He deftly back-heeled the ball for his teammate but Tosin managed to thump it clear. Bamford felt the need to offer an explanation to Llorente and, nodding in Roberts' direction, he said "I heard him shout!"

There were occasions when Bamford's unselfishness was not for the best and this was one of them.

Soon it looked bad; Patrick Bamford was hobbling; the only good thing was, when the physios came on to treat him, it wasn't a recurrence of the hip injury which forced him off against Chelsea-the painkilling spray went on his shins.

In the twenty-nineth minute, Bamford, who'd failed to score in three successive matches pounced unerringly on a fine cross from Harrison and smote it home first touch. Typically modest, he admitted, in the post-match interview, that the ball had gone in off his shin.

Pumped up by his strike, Bamford tripped Cavaleiro a minute afterwards. David Coote, indulgent of Fulham infringements, showed no leniency, promptly brandishing a yellow card.

Fed by Phillips in the 57th minute, Bamford evaded Anderson's wild lunge and slipped a fine ball beyond Tosin to Raphinha; Raphinha nonchalantly shrugged off Tete and prodded the ball into the back of the net. Two outstanding Leeds players, the quick thinking Patrick Bamford and Raphinha, a marvel of agility and balance, embraced joyfully.

70 minutes gone and Patrick Bamford, fed up with Anderson's fouling, tripped the lanky Lyon loanee and was at once shame-faced, realising that, with one booking to his name, he'd risked dismissal –and with it a three match suspension. Fortunately, Mr Coote's leniency worked in Leeds' favour this time.

Nevertheless Marcelo Bielsa was furious. On the opposite touchline he cupped his hand over his mouth turning it into a megaphone as he shouted "BAMFOR!–no more that!!!" Patrick's face turned ashen and a couple of minutes later he failed to stop the ball going over the touchline. His boss decided to reprieve him and bring him off in favour of Klich.

For 75 minutes Patrick Bamford was below his best in the home game against Liverpool. First he made a complete mess of his shot as Harrison delivered a fine freekick. Then, after a mistake from Fabinho gifted the ball to Kalvin Phillips, Phillips promptly found him but his first touch was weak and Firmino was able to save the day.

Then he suddenly sprang into life when Ayling found him in the D with a long high ball. Bamford's delicate high trap brought the ball down. Completely confounding Arnold with his aplomb, he waited for the ball to bounce then lobbed it clean over Alisson's head with a powerful left foot half volley. Sadly his sheer brilliance went unrewarded; the ball crashed back off the lower crossbar rebounding fully fifteen yards before Liverpool managed to get it clear.

Patrick Bamford's technique in this moment was, even though he narrowly failed to score, on another level from the perfectly good goal he registered at Anfield. Interviewed after the match he admitted his disappointment at not scoring. Had he executed a similarly impressive but unsuccessful shot at Anfield, he would have been delighted. This was a mark of his progress across seven months of a Premiership season. He'd moved from being a player about whom the pundits were still sceptical to a first-class centre forward now recognised by everyone except Southgate as a potentially effective striker on the international stage.

Away at Southampton, Patrick Bamford was the central figure in a controversial incident following a great Leeds' counter-attack. Dallas had found Raphinha clear on the touchline, the Brazilian had sized up the situation at one forward glance to deliver a fine curling ball beyond Vestergaard bouncing straight into Bamford's path. Goalkeeper McCarthy was nonplussed by the speed of the move, he ran out of his area then dodged back. When Bamford touched the ball wide of him, McCarthy tried to grab hold of his ankle causing the Leeds' centre forward to stagger. Most strikers would undoubtedly have gone to ground on first feeling such a contact yet Bamford, totally honest, continued. This enabled Vestergaard to catch up with him and get the ball out for a corner.

Bamford strode at once grim-faced towards Peter Bankes, posing a question which the referee could not answer –"do I have to dive?" Without doubt Mr Bankes should have awarded a penalty the moment he saw Bamford staggering from McCarthy's foul.

Not long afterwards, attempting a stooping header from Harrison's cross, Bamford stumbled into the blameless Salisu and fell to the turf barely moving.There was a lengthy hiatus while the physios rushed on to attend to him, during which Marcelo Bielsa was given permission from the fourth official for a concussion substitution. Mercifully Patrick revived, the physios were satisfied that he was not concussed and he continued.

A happier outcome followed in the 72nd minute when Bamford, fed with a fantastic chip from Rodrigo which took out four Southampton players, tapped the ball clear of McCarthy for the opening goal.

One of the most significant features of the Southampton game was Patrick Bamford's sportsmanship, in his appropriately immaculate white shirt, which testified to a Leeds' squad inculcated with Marcelo Bielsa's ethical standards gaining a fully deserved victory.

Against West Bromwich Albion on May 23 Patrick Bamford scored his 17th goal of the season, a penalty. Playing only the second half he was acclaimed by 8000 Elland Road fans with the chant "England's Number One!" Two days later, however, Bamford was excluded from the 33 man provisional squad chosen by Gareth Southgate for Euro 2021. With the exception of Harry Kane, he'd scored more Premiership goals than any other English striker. What's more, he was known to be an unselfish player who frequently laid on assists for his club teammates and he'd remained free from injury throughout the season. The question could not be evaded: what was it about Patrick Bamford which stopped Southgate selecting him?

THE SKIPPER

LIAM COOPER

"Cooper is a huge part of this club" said Marcelo Bielsa, dismissing speculation that Leeds' main centre back would leave after Diego Llorente was bought. "I'm referring to the patrimony between him and the institution" he elaborated before, sensing that the interpreter wasn't rendering his cultured Spanish into everyday English, he added "he's someone who always behaves in an impeccable manner."

Elaborating further on another occasion, Bielsa characterised Cooper as "an exceptional captain, someone who cares about the welfare of others rather than about himself" adding "he generously helps others and he's humble about seeking help for himself."

Bielsa knew that character is an even more important attribute in a player than ball skill, shooting power and a football brain. And at Elland Road it was the three British players who'd come up unsung the hard way –Cooper, Ayling and Dallas –who were the beating heart of the team. Bielsa recognised that probably from the get go and certainly after their devastated reaction when

Leeds didn't make it out of the Championship under him at the first attempt.

Unlike Luke Ayling, Liam Cooper isn't an extrovert. He's a modest guy not given to showing off. Yet his level gaze is that of a real warrior –'don't mess with me' is what it says to an opponent. Back in the day Cooper would have been described as 'a man among men', the kind of talk which no mainstream pundit would dare utter nowadays for fear of being cancelled for Woke bollocks about so-called 'toxic masculinity.' But when he hoisted Leeds' own IBF featherweight champion Josh Warrington on his shoulders to celebrate the Whites' return to their rightful place in the Premiership, this was exactly what Liam Cooper was.

Harshly rejected by his hometown club Hull City, loaned to a couple of Division One clubs, Carlisle United and Huddersfield Town, Cooper was sold to Chesterfield with whom he remained in Division 2 for a couple of seasons. He arrived at Elland Road in the summer of 2014 having impressed in a preseason friendly.

While a minority of Leeds' fans scoffed at deficiencies in Liam's technique, manager Neil Redfearn did not. What's more, he recognised him quickly as a strong character, both liked and respected in the dressing room, and made him club captain.

Reflecting on his career in an interview with the Telegraph, Cooper said "it was an emotional time for me when I was told I had to leave Hull. But it's how you overcome adversity that defines you as a man, let alone a footballer." He added "I'm from a working class family and my dad taught me to never give up."

Chatting with Josh Warrington for a Leeds documentary, footballer and boxer were soon on the same wavelength. "You know what it means with Leeds –working class!" said Josh as Liam nodded.

Here was the heart of the matter as far as both club and city are concerned. Despised by the London media for decade after decade, unjustly accused of all manner of sins, the unequalled zeal of their fans testifies to a sense of outrage.

Liam himself has made clear the difference between his attitude and its opposite, machismo. Never did he show this more clearly than when he adopted 13 year old cancer battler Elliot Metcalfe as a virtual mascot. Elliot was zoomed into Liam's iPad just as Leeds and Arsenal lined up in front of the cameras before kick-off. Though Leeds played Arsenal off the park, the match ended in a nil nil draw. Cooper's first reaction afterwards was that "I was sorry I couldn't get three points for the lad."

Before promotion Liam Cooper's goals for the club could've been counted on the fingers of two hands. So it was all the more important that, with Leeds 4-0 down at Old Trafford and, as the pundits reckoned, all set for total humiliation, he stepped up to the plate with a cracker from a corner, a sharply angled bullet header which gave world class keeper de Gea not a hope in hell. Given the state of the game, Cooper didn't celebrate but the "yeah!" he muttered to himself as he jogged away testified to his quiet satisfaction that he could cut the mustard at this level.

As the season progressed Liam Cooper remained undaunted by the injuries which had struck down his intended central defensive partners, Robin Koch and Diego Llorente. Then, from around the turn of the year, he worked steadfastly in tandem with Pascal Struijk and their comfortable inter-passing surprised many opponents who expected Leeds to surge into all out attack from the word go. The flow of goals conceded was stemmed except at the Emirates where, in a rare strategic misjudgement by Bielsa, Struijk was deployed in midfield.

Leeds' skipper was the focus of attention in an impertinent postmatch interview following the narrow defeat at the Molineux Stadium. BT Sport's Matt Smith snidely remarked "your captain should have had a hat-trick!" Marcelo Bielsa didn't dignify such ignorance with a response.

Co-commentator and former Leeds United and England women's international, the astute and fair-minded Lucy Ward had already pointed out that, whilst Cooper had been at fault with a misdirected header from a perfectly dropping Raphinha free kick, his point blank header, though hit straight at Rui Patricio, was powerful enough to have beaten most keepers. As for Liam's full stretch shot, it was only kept out by a world-class save from the Wolverhampton keeper which left the Whites' skipper shaking his head in utter disbelief!

Until the 44th minute of the match against Manchester City at the Etihad, Liam Cooper was going great guns. He had Gabriel Jesus in his pocket and the block he'd made after being shouldered to the ground at a corner saved a certain goal. But a lapse of concentration from both Luke Ayling and himself gave Jesus the chance to dart forward –before Cooper's thunderous tackle deposited him on the deck.

At first referee Andre Marriner contented himself with a yellow card. After all, Liam had got the ball, hooking it high into touch. Then VAR operative David Coote intervened, advising the ref to look at the monitor. As he did so, BT cameras focused on Jesus lying prone receiving medical attention interspersed with a barrage of slomo replays of Leeds' skipper's challenge. After the ref showed red, Jesus got to his feet clearly none the worse for wear and Cooper insisted, even as he walked off, "I got the fuckin' ball!"

The skipper's dismissal proved to be the turning point in the match but not in the way the pundits predicted. Far from it, Marcelo Bielsa reorganised the remaining ten men in an unprecedented low block which brought about a stunning victory.

Liam Cooper was then suspended for three matches and, in his absence Pascal Struijk partnered Diego Llorente in Leeds' rearguard. Returning for the final game of the season he reappeared alongside Gaetano Berardi, a man who, like Liam, had been an absolute stalwart in the Whites' central defence.

THE ENIGMA

HELDER COSTA

At the start of the season, Helder Costa's loan from Wolverhampton was confirmed as a permanent deal for an undisclosed sum reported to be around £16 million.

A Championship regular albeit a rare goalscorer, Helder Costa had a mixed game in Leeds' first Premiership match, at Liverpool. He had the ball in the net early doors but was correctly given offside. He would have been well placed to benefit from Phillips and Harrison's fine approach work had he not strayed offside again. Indeed he was bawled out by Marcelo Bielsa for lack of awareness when he did that. Costa was, however, well alert to exploit Robertson's slack marking when he produced a fine low bouncing cross for Klich's equalising goal.

The other side of the coin was, however, his modest workrate. Compared to the assistance Harrison was giving Dallas in subduing Arnold, he gave Ayling relatively little help in stopping Robertson's runs.

Helder Costa entered club history when he became the first man to score a Premiership goal at Elland Road after the 16 year hiatus, cracking home a fine angled shot. He followed up with a sprightly second after a fine cutback from Bamford.

At home to Manchester City, Costa was shaken up by fouls from their hefty French full-back Benjamin Mendy but, when Bielsa switched him to the other flank at half-time, he was often too clever for Kyle Walker.

Costa showed up well below his best when visiting Molyneux, the home of his old club, Wolves. He failed to profit from an excellent buildup by Dallas and Bamford, screwing his shot yards wide when well placed. He later scuffed another shot after being supplied by Bamford via Harrison.

Helder Costa's fluctuating form continued with an improvement at Villa Park where he assisted Patrick Bamford's third goal with a shrewd pass. Away against Palace, however, his streaky deflection of a van Aanholt shot left Meslier helpless.

Slowly but surely Marcelo Bielsa was preparing Raphinha, signed on the last day of the transfer window in October, to take over from Helder Costa on the right wing and, after Raphinha's brilliant full debut against Arsenal on November 22, Costa became little more than an understudy to the Brazilian.

He began to lose focus thereafter and, less often selected to play for Portugal's excellent side, he opted to represent Angola instead. While some commended his allegiance to the land of his birth, more sceptical critics wondered whether he was looking for a relatively easy ride.

Helder Costa was of course well capable of playing on either wing and Bielsa gave him a second chance when Jack Harrison suffered a loss of form early in the second half of the season.

Coming on for the second half at the Emirates, with Leeds facing heavy defeat, he pulled one goal back when, fed by Roberts, he swerved past Xaka and scored. This was his first strike since his brace against Fulham and was a reminder of his abilities.

Once again replacing Harrison at half-time against Southampton, Helder Costa played with unusual energy, on one occasion sprinting back to foil the dangerous Tella and dispossessing him at the cost of a corner from which nothing came. Later, still working hard, he registered an assist for Dallases' goal. Few knew what might have prompted this apparent transformation. Had Costa felt unwanted after Raphinha emerged? Did he now think that a new door had opened for him with Harrison's loss of form? Costa remained an enigma.

Preferred to Harrison from the outset for the visit of Aston Villa, Costa was badly at fault for El Ghazi's early goal, being slow to react to the danger from Watkins' cross. From then he could do little right and this time, on the hour, it was Harrison replacing him. It wasn't long before Harrison was looking like his old self once again producing a glorious last-minute cross from which Raphinha ought to have scored.

Surprisingly preferred by Bielsa to Harrison for the away game against West Ham, Costa seemed reluctant to put himself about against the physical Hammers and was taken off in favour of the English lad at half-time.

Harrison looked fully reintegrated in the next few games but circumstances gave Helder Costa a further opportunity due to the rival winger being ineligible against his parent club, Manchester City.

Given an earful at close quarters from Marcelo Bielsa, Costa promptly bucked himself up and, assisted by a lucky rebound, got the better of Cancelo. Then his ball to Bamford began the move which led to Dallas' first goal. And for Stuart's memorable stoppage time winner, it was Costa who found Alioski to supply the crucial pass.

Helder Costa got yet another chance to redeem himself when Raphinha's injury at the end of the match with Manchester City prevented him from appearing against Liverpool. But Costa didn't take it. Early on he was caught napping when Robertson was played through with a good pass. Fortunately the Scotsman failed to take advantage of the error.

Next Costa was well found by Tyler Roberts' crossfield ball but, though he started to dribble, he soon lost control. After that Costa's indolence vis-à-vis his teammates showed up more and more and though he remained on the pitch for over an hour, this was probably due to Marcelo Bielsa's lack of faith in Ian Poveda. When Poveda finally came on to replace Costa, he did more in the remaining time than the Angolan had done in 67 minutes.

When Leeds faced Manchester United at home, Raphinha had still not been able to resume training after his injury against Man City. In the circumstances Marcelo Bielsa was obliged to persist with Helder Costa.

But it wasn't long before Costa was staggering after a fair shoulder charge from Luke Shaw. It was all too obvious he wasn't strong enough to cope with the man he was supposed to be marking.

Then when Dallases' clever play had baffled Wan-Bissaka, Costa found himself in the clear but could only misplace his pass ahead of Bamford. Much the same thing happened when Struijk made a good clearance and simultaneously found Costa with a fine pass only for the Angolan to lose control.

Switched to the opposite wing by Marcelo Bielsa at half-time, Costa had a fine opportunity when Kalvin Phillips sent him clear with a crossfield ball. He lashed a shot but Wan-Bissaka flicked out a foot and deflected the ball onto the roof of the net with Henderson stranded.

Later Costa was subjected to a fierce wrestling-style challenge by Wan-Bissaka. Disadvantaged by bodyweight, the fragile winger was hurled to the floor and required extensive treatment. Badly shaken up, he had to be replaced by Klich and was out of action for the rest of the season.

THE MASTER OF MURDER BALL

STUART DALLAS

At Stuart Dallas' grammar school in Cookstown, Northern Ireland, the emphasis was on hockey not football. Fortunately the Dallas family played a big part in running the local intermediate club, Coagh United. From there Stuart went on to play for Crusaders and thence to Brentford before arriving at Leeds in 2015. His transfer fee, a mere £1.3 million, was a fantastic example of money well spent.

Articulate and intelligent, Dallas is a natural for interviews. Yet when he's in front of a mic, he's likely to say unexpected things. Acknowledging that he was a boyhood Liverpool supporter, he dismissed the misconception that, in Northern Ireland, fans of the Premiership invariably support either the Reds or Manchester United. Far from it, he made it clear that Leeds have a big following in Cookstown.

A guy with a sharp sense of humour, Stuart Dallas smiled at how some fans acclaimed the squad which won the Championship as 'legends' only to assume they'd automatically carry all before them in the Premiership. But far from shirking pressure, he said the more of it there was the better. Fan pressure was what made you play better especially when you could hear it loud and clear at Elland Road.

As soon as Marcelo Bielsa arrived at Leeds in 2018, the players became accustomed to video analysis of their upcoming opponents. That wasn't per se a novelty–most top-flight clubs practiced it. But it soon became crystal clear that Bielsa knew everything there was to know about every other club in the Championship. As soon as Derby County's Frank Lampard insinuated malpractice in the so-called 'Spygate' affair, Bielsa brushed the charge aside in an unforgettable analysis designed to put the media straight. Everyone at Elland Road was impressed by the manager's intellect and none more so than Stuart Dallas.

Dallas was to benefit even more from Marcelo Bielsa's insistence on exceptional physical fitness. It wasn't him who christened these hyper-demanding sessions 'murder ball'–it was either Luke Ayling or Kalvin Phillips –but Dallas was the one who emerged from them with a standard of fitness second to none. You could see this as plain as plain can be whenever he sprinted 40 yards on overlap and scarcely needed to catch his breath.

"Marcelo pushes you so hard in training that, at the beginning, you're on the verge of vomiting. But when match day comes around, you're so fit you feel like you're flying."These are the words of Spanish international Ander Herrera who played for Bielsa at Athletic Bilbao. But Stuart Dallas would doubtless endorse the sentiments.

Dallas' tackling was distinctly old school and he could fall foul of some referees in that regard. Had these whistlers ever officiated in a match involving Billy Bremner or Johnny Giles they'd have likely come out in a cold sweat!

Like Cooper and Ayling, Dallas is a stalwart man. But technically he's more reliable than Liam and Luke. What's more, he scores goals! His first Premiership strike came against Leicester at home when the Foxes trounced the Whites 4-1. Just about the only bright spot for Leeds that day was Stuart's speculative shot from long range which deceived Kasper Schmeichel.

In total contrast Dallas regained the lead for the Peacocks against Newcastle setting them on their way to a crushing 5-2 victory. This time he snuck in unmarked to score with a stooping header.

Stuart Dallas has played a total of 46 games for Northern Ireland including those at Euro 2016. He has no fear whatever of the big time and demonstrated this perfectly in the game against Manchester United at Old Trafford when pundits asserted that Leeds had taken a hammering. Finding himself on the receiving end of a 6-1 scoreline which grossly exaggerated the gap between the two sides, Dallas strode imperturbably on, not to register some sort of so-called consolation but to strike a great goal. Perfectly anticipating the buildup in which Jack Harrison's well flighted long high pass was instantly tapped back to him by Raphina, he calmly waited a moment for a gap to appear in United's shaky defence and, when it did, he smote an unstoppable shot beyond de Gea into the far top corner of the net.

It was a goal of a very different kind which the Ulsterman scored at the King Power Stadium to cancel Leicester's lead within a couple of minutes of them establishing it. Though his characteristic fitness and pitch coverage put him perfectly in position to collect Patrick Bamford's delicate assist, he relied on a close range cleverly angled shot beyond Schmeichel to put Leeds back on even terms.

When Harrison made the score 3-1 against the Foxes, Dallas played a key part in the build-up, adroitly picking up Struik's headed clearance and shoulder charging a Leicester lad aside before he cleverly picked out Klich who went on to feed Harrison via Bamford.

Stuart Dallas showed all his qualities as both a footballer and a man in the home game against Southampton. Picking up a quick clearance from Luke Ayling he brilliantly bisected Saints' two most dangerous players, Ward-Prowse and Romeu with a levered pass which sent Raphinha clean through only to be foiled by Romeu's astounding recovery tackle.

It was Dallas who did most to clinch victory when, picked out by a clever ball from Pablo Hernandez, he swapped passes with Helder Costa before cracking his shot well beyond McCarthy. Andy Hinchcliffe of BT Sport seemed to be debunking this with a snide comment about "a toe poke." Stuart's goal may not have been elegant but it was crucial.

Dallas was anxious to commemorate the passing of Val Crosby, Kalvin Phillips' beloved grandmother and a lady who, as a Leeds supporter from way back when, had featured notably in the documentary 'Take Us Home.' Well aware of instructions to referees to book any player removing his shirt, he'd arranged with Pablo Quiroga to receive a replica White shirt with the words 'Granny Val' inscribed and he made sure the club's tribute captured the attention of Sky cameras.

It was a gesture typical of Stuart, a man of firm family values who married his teenage sweetheart and long-term girlfriend Juneve Lamont with whom he has three young children.

For all his indefatigable work rate and his goals, Dallas was receiving little recognition from the media for his contribution to Leeds' successes. Had Stuart been an Englishman, they'd have been demanding his inclusion in Southgate's squad. As it was, he came in handy for post-match interviews where he could be relied on to comment intelligently in his distinctive brogue.

Last but by no means least, Stuart Dallas' versatility is a highlight of his game and one much valued by Marcelo Bielsa who's deployed him variously at right back, left back, in midfield and on the right wing.

Stuart Dallas was the hero of the hour when Leeds took down City at the Etihad. All his qualities were on display –his unquenchable energy, his sheer will to win and his capacity for clinical finishing particularly on the big occasion. His brace comprised his bolt from the blue impeccably placed opener and, in stoppage time, his almost impudent nutmeg which bewildered the Brazilian Ederson, hailed by many as the world's best keeper.

The BT staffer who interviewed Dallas after the match naively commented that Leeds never seem to give up was met with Stuart's frowning response- "you should never give up whoever you play for!"

Ever ready to fulfil any role required of him by Marcelo Bielsa, Stuart Dallas became a right winger at home against Spurs. Within a dozen minutes he scored, pouncing on Lloris' parry and cracking the ball into the roof of the net. Maintaining his incredible energy to the very end, he was only denied a second by an exceptional Lloris' save.

At the conclusion of the season Stuart Dallas was voted Player of the Year by Leeds' fans. It was an honour richly deserved.

FROM BOLTON VIA MASSACHUSETTS AND MANHATTAN

JACK HARRISON

"Mum, I just love it over here!" With these words 14 year old Jack Harrison sought to reassure his mother that her decision to let him go to the USA on a football scholarship was the right one. Debbie Harrison was an astute and farsighted lady, a PA at a law firm in Bolton. Her son seemed destined for a football career when she saw him kicking a ball almost as soon as he could walk. Jack had been a starstruck lad on the books of Manchester United but his mum pointed out to him group photographs on the walls at Old Trafford of previous Academy teams. "Where are those boys now?" she said, adding "do you recognise any of them?"

Jack was an intelligent lad and his mother was anxious that he shouldn't disregard his education and leave himself unqualified if his career in professional football didn't materialise. So off he went to Berkshire College in Massachusetts and from there he obtained a place at Wake Forest University in Winston-Salem. Jack left Wake after only six months not because he was struggling with the course but because he'd secured an offer from Chicago Fire in the MLS. From Chicago he was soon traded to New York City and at the age of 19 was playing alongside such great footballers as Andrea Pirlo and David Villa under the management of Patrick Vieira. His precocious skill was soon saluted by all three of them thus preparing the way for a return home to sister club Manchester City two years later.

City were scarcely noted for patiently nurturing young Englishmen and, six months later, Jack Harrison went on loan to Leeds. This coincided with the arrival at Elland Road of Marcelo Bielsa.

Harrison soon realised that in Bielsa he had a coach who was, to all intents and purposes, an unrivalled professor of football. Bielsa, for his part, quickly noted a young man not only highly skilful but a dedicated student eager to learn.

Successive seasons on loan led to a proposed deal halfway through the 2020-21 season wherein Leeds would pay City over £10 million for Harrison's transfer. Were this to be finalized it would be a shrewd piece of business since his value on the open market would likely be at least four times that amount. True, Harrison's goals were more spectacular than frequent but, deployed as a left winger, he assisted many strikes with his pinpoint crosses not to mention his perseverance in the face of rugged challenges and his dedication to tracking back.

The opening match of the season, on September 12, saw him score a fantastic goal at Anfield against Champions Liverpool. As a boy in Stoke he dreamt of doing exactly that except in a red shirt not a white one. His dad was a keen Liverpool supporter but, when his parents went their separate ways, Jack returned with his mum to Lancashire and fell under the sway of Manchester United.

Leeds' first Premiership goal of the Bielsa era stemmed from Kalvin Phillips' superb pass to Jack Harrison. Harrison's ball control was phenomenal and his face was a mask of concentration as he brushed aside Alexander-Arnold and Gomez before leaving Alisson stunned as the Whites' left-winger's shot flew past him. And Reds' captain Virgil van Dijk looked aghast that someone who was only a name to him had the effrontery to execute such a goal. Strangely, Harrison himself looked almost shocked after he'd found the net as if he could scarcely believe that he'd cancelled the Reds' lead at a stroke.

Marcelo Bielsa's reaction was unequivocal. He rose from his mobile bucket and punched the air in joy not only at the fact of the equaliser but the way in which it was conceived and executed by two players he personally transformed –Phillips' intelligence and precision and Jack Harrison's tremendous skill and sangfroid.

Everything seemed set for Jack Harrison's transformation into a lethal winger/striker. But in actual fact it would be three full months before he found the net again. Paradoxically for a thoughtful player it seemed the more time he had to think the more it put him off. A case in point came against Everton at Goodison Park after only 10 minutes. After Raphina's fantastic 40 yard run, he passed to Harrison who was unmarked 10 yards out with only the keeper to beat. The pass was perfection with the ball rolling to a stop at Jack's foot. But incredibly he placed it just wide of the post. Mortified by his miss, he briefly lay prostrate covering his face with his hands.

Fortunately the error didn't cost Leeds the match since Raphina eventually fired the winner. But, aside from poor finishing, Harrison was going through a bad patch around this time. The previous season he cancelled his Twitter account after receiving a torrent of abuse from moronic Manc fans who picked on him because he'd left their Academy nine years earlier. There was never anything like that from Leeds supporters but there were some on social media who wondered whether Harrison had been distracted by his beautiful girlfriend, the Costa Rican model Fiorella Arbenz.

In actual fact Jack Harrison was dedicated to improving his game. "I'm my own worst critic" he said, admitting that he was prone to nitpick but adding that perseverance was the epitome of the complete footballer.

Fortified by Bielsa's faith in him, Harrison confounded the doubters by scoring another wonderful goal, this time at home against Newcastle United on December 16. With the score at 4-2 for Leeds and only three minutes left, it was the icing on the cake. Still, it was unforgettable.

Jack's goal saw him combine all the elements of a great footballer –skill, pace, vision and shooting power. He began with an instantaneous trap of Pablo Hernandez' clever pass; checking for an instant to see Mateusz Klich on a parallel run, he opted not to use him but to set off on a fast jinking run which flummoxed the Newcastle defenders. From 25 yards out he took barely a moment to adjust his radar before sending the ball hurtling into the top corner of the net.

Three games later Jack Harrison was on the scoresheet again, against West Bromwich at The Hawthorns. Once again it was no ordinary goal but an audacious piece of football ballet. Facing the doughty Furlong in the box he executed a stunning sequence –left foot trap, right foot cushion, deliberate disconcerting delay, heel tap and swerve, dropped shoulder and an impudent chip beyond top class keeper Sam Johnstone high into the top corner, 0-3.

Rodrigo and Raphina were the first to congratulate their teammate. Who said Englishmen can't show incredible skill? These two know different. Harrison digs Brazilian music when the pair of them play it in the dressing room, now he'd scored a goal which would have brought the house down at Maracana. Referring to Rodrigo and Raphina, he described them as "both really happy people" before concluding "you can build a real chemistry with them –based on camaraderie not competition."

Harrison and Raphina linked up again at St James Park in January with the pass and shot which concluded a seven man move beginning almost on the Leeds' dead ball line. Harrison, unmarked but wide left called for the ball and Raphina delivered it with a wonderful lofted pass, half dinked, half floated. Harrison executed an instant thigh trap then showed consummate skill as he curled his shot with the outside of his left foot beyond the diving Darlow aiming and finding the far corner to send the ball in off the post. It came at a vital stage of the game putting Newcastle back in their place after they'd equalised only four minutes earlier.

After four superb strikes, Harrison was on the scoresheet again at the King Power Stadium. This time it was a tap in after Patrick Bamford had raced half the length of the pitch and seemed poised to score. Yet with Harrison unmarked wide of him, Bamford played him in with a square pass. His face wreathed in smiles, Jack pointed to Patrick, saluting his unselfishness.

Jack Harrison's comments about his Brazilian buddies really sum him up. In some ways he seems quintessentially English, his cheery grin alternating with beetle-browed determination as he rides the rugged tackles. When he speaks, his Lancashire accent's remained intact despite his teenage years in the States. But from another point of view he's become cosmopolitan, at ease with his Latin teammates and delighted with his Central American girlfriend.

Sadly Jack's innate good nature was exploited by BT Sport in an interview before the unlucky defeat by Wolves where he ingenuously allowed himself to be enmeshed in their foolish narrative about 'Leeds the Entertainers.' He was not at his best during the game and on one occasion failed to stop running the ball out over the touchline. What might have seemed to the casual observer like poor technique was in fact down to the fact that it was blowing half a gale in the Midlands that night!

Off form against Southampton where he was subbed at half time and benched against Aston Villa to give Helder Costa a chance at redemption, he proved once he came on in the Villa game that he was far superior with a sumptuous running cross which he curled over Mings and Targett and from which Raphinha should have headed the equaliser.

Starting against Chelsea, Harrison aimed to find Bamford with a wonderful dipping cross only to be foiled by Rudiger's stupendous clearance by means of a near-horizontal diving header. Surprisingly subbed in favour of Costa -whose workrate left much to be desired- Jack trudged off the pitch with a gesture of bewilderment.

Harrison was right back to his best form against Fulham at Craven Cottage. His was the assist for Bamford's goal. It resulted from a fine low cross levered into the goalmouth after he ignored a crude attempt at intimidation from the Nigerian, Ola Aina.

Later Jack jinked past Anguissa and Ola Aina and boldly tried a shot on the angle which Areola saved. He was man enough to acknowledge, with an apologetic raised arm, a complaint from Tyler Roberts that he, being unmarked, should have received a pass.

By now Fulham had completely shot their bolt, outwitted by sheer skill and knackered by a far greater fitness level. Harrison was in his absolute element, swerving away from Loftus-Cheek so bewilderingly that the lanky loanee from Lewisham lost his balance even trying to get near him and staggered to the turf in disarray.

Loftus-Cheek ended up in Mr Coote's book soon afterwards, hunting Harrison; it was a borderline sending off checked by VAR but not confirmed.

In interview Jack attributed his return to form to the benefits of motivational counselling from a practitioner of neurolinguistic programming. Leeds fans couldn't have cared less one way or the other about NLP provided Harrison was banging the ball into the back of the net. He hadn't done this for a couple of months but, 12 minutes into the game with Sheffield United, he did. To be more exact, he prodded home from a mere 2 yards out after being brilliantly set up by a superb pass from Raphinha.

In the absence of Raphinha against Liverpool at Elland Road, the burden of mounting attacks down the wings fell heavily on Jack Harrison especially with Helder Costa proving a dud on the opposite flank. Jack responded with a superb display. First, he delivered a pinpoint free kick which put Bamford in with an excellent chance of scoring only for the centre forward to make a mess of his shot. Then he placed a perfect cut back to Tyler Roberts only for Roberts to shoot straight at the keeper.

It was a matter of character as well as skill with Harrison. Just turned the hour he spoiled a good move involving Llorente and Roberts by badly overhitting a cross far beyond Bamford. Head down, grimacing and muttering, he was very disappointed with himself over this continuing weakness in his game.

Determined to atone for his blunder, he fired himself up to do that at the first available opportunity. He looked a world-class player with his superb dribble and shot as he surged into the six yard box. He evaded Milner's lunging tackle, swerved away from Fabinho and angled his shot seemingly leaving Alisson without a chance. Yet Alisson, the world's best keeper, foiled him by an instantaneous parry with his extended left foot. Harrison was only denied by a rebound which spun inches beyond his boot as it went out of play. He clasped his hands to the back of his head in sheer disbelief at having been deprived of another superb goal to add to the ones he'd already scored during the season.

With four minutes left on the clock Jack Harrison delivered a wonderful inswinging corner which confounded the Liverpool defence and resulted in a headed goal for Diego Llorente. After the match Marcelo Bielsa, in a rare departure from his norm of spreading praise equally between his players, picked out Harrison for a special commendation.

Jack Harrison was a thorn in Spurs' side from first minute to last when the Londoners came to Elland Road. He was the chief creator of Leeds' opening goal when he humiliated Aurier before clipping a dropping cross through the six yard box. Dier couldn't handle it and Reguilon made a bollocks of it, Hugo Lloris did his best to keep it out but could only parry for Stuart Dallas to score.

Next, demonstrating his ambidextrous skill, Harrison changed feet in the blink of an eye after leaving Aurier floundering in his wake. His fearsome right footed shot would have been too much for most keepers and it took a world class save from Lloris to keep it out.

Well and truly pumped up, Jack left all his early season undue deference behind him when he upbraided the purple-shirted Premiership prime referee Michael Oliver bawling "what for?" when the Geordie whistler blew him up for a foul against the shamelessly shamming Aurier.

Early in the second half, when Marcelo Bielsa brought Raphinha on, Harrison was switched to the right where he coped as contemptuously with Reguilon as he already had with Aurier.

After the match, the pundits were singing Harrison's praises and Steve McManaman went into raptures about "this kid's fabulous two-footed skill." "He's good enough to be playin' for a top four team" McManaman raved. The Scouser seemed to have no comprehension that, following Leeds' massive improvement in the second half of the season, they were effectively a top four team themselves. Careless talk such as this only emphasised the importance of Victor Orta swiftly turning Harrison's Manchester City loan into a permanent move to Elland Road.

Jack Harrison had a great game against Burnley at Turf Moor, stunning the Claret and Blues with his high skill and tenacity. He was right on target with Leeds' second when he reacted like lightning to Alioski's shot from Dallases' corner and executed an impudent backheel flick which diverted it beyond the stranded Peacock - Farrell. Harrison grinned widely but didn't celebrate. It seemed as if he thought he simply got lucky yet Marcelo Bielsa reckoned otherwise. Rubbing his hands in delight at Harrison's insouciance, he later characterised it as "a beautiful goal."

Later Harrison was at the heart of the buildup for both Rodrigo's goals. For the first he picked up a good header from Struijk and, spotting space between the two centre backs, he steered a lance-like pass to the Spaniard as he moved into the D. For the second, he made a great pass beyond Charlie Taylor to find Rodrigo once again too quick and clever for Burnley to resist.

Despite having scored eight Premiership goals as a winger and providing eight assists, Harrison was excluded from Southgate's provisional England squad for Euro 2021. Nevertheless on the last day of the season he scored a perfectly good goal against West Bromwich only to have it chalked off by ref David Coote because he deemed their keeper was distracted by Rodrigo. 8000 Leeds' fans responded by chanting Jack's name. Southgate didn't rate him but they most certainly did!

ARRIBA LA BAMBA!

PABLO HERNANDEZ

Many fans were saddened when Pablo Hernandez was super-seded by Rodrigo as season 2020-1 got going. It wasn't like they had anything against Rodrigo and indeed they recognised that, at his best, the Brazilian-born Spaniard was a world-class player. It was just that during the lean years they'd taken Hernandez to their hearts as the epitome of skill combined with rugged determina-tion. It may have helped that the guy from Valencia had homely features –a bruiser's mug if truth be told. When he first appeared in Josh Warrington's corner in October 2019, he didn't look out of place in the slightest and indeed the roar which went up from the crowd testified to his popularity. And when artist Adrian Duffield painted a spectacular mural celebrating Pablo Hernandez' goal against Swansea City which clinched promotion, he found sup-porters standing in worshipful admiration before the wall by the 'Dog and Duck.' Sadly it proved to be the writing on the wall as far as Hernandez' career was concerned.

Pablo's performances in the Premiership didn't match up to what he'd achieved in earlier seasons in the Championship -

the fantastic free kicks, the impudent lobs, the strikes perfectly delivered to the far top corner, the three hundred chances created! At 35 years of age this was scarcely surprising. Yet it culminated in his petulant reaction after being substituted against Leicester City which led to his being disciplined the following week when he was not included, despite being fully fit, in the squad which travelled to London to face Crystal Palace. Pablo saw the need to apologise to Marcelo Bielsa. He did so and was reintegrated.

In the Premiership Pablo Hernandez was best used as an impact substitute in the late stages of a game when his legs were still fresh. Against Newcastle he achieved two important assists in the space of 10 minutes, notably his clever pass from deep which sent Jack Harrison away to score his wonder goal.

Brought on against Everton with a quarter of an hour left and Leeds desperately seeking an equaliser, Pablo Hernandez produced a brilliant cameo which came close to turning the tide. First, he adroitly found Bamford in the D but Patrick, who'd never had service as good as that all night, reacted with surprise and failed to control the ball.

Next, after Bielsa switched Raphinha to the left, Hernandez played him in with a pinpoint pass only for Holgate to stop him with as blatant a piece of shirt pulling as you're ever likely to see. When Mr Oliver booked him, there was no reaction from Holgate, he was still busy chomping on chewy- his only concern was to thwart Leeds' Latin artists by all means necessary.

When Philips' freekick was headed away, Dallas pounced on it and slipped the ball instantly to Hernandez. Pablo prompted Ayling in a move which finished when Raphinha overhit his cross for a goal kick. Five minutes stoppage time were signalled and Mr Oliver booked Olsen for blatant time wasting. Essentially Everton had been panicked into infringements by the threat from Hernandez' deadly skilful passing.

Finally, with only half a minute left on the clock, the tireless Stuart Dallas took over and found Bamford. Hernandez immediately pointed out that the Toffees had unaccountably left Tyler Roberts completely free, standing just inside the area. Bamford's excellent pass went straight to the feet of the Welshman but, with all the time in the world to strike for goal, he walloped the ball high over the bar, covering his face in mortification. It was the kind of chance which Pablo Hernandez in his prime would have instantly despatched into the far top corner of the net.

Given half-an-hour not a mere 15 minutes to make an impact, against Wolves at the Molineux Stadium, Pablo Hernandez' skill, intelligence and savvy were there for all to see. Had Patrick Bamford's devastating finish not been nullified by VAR nonsense, Hernandez would have had a pre-assist. Lying deep in his own half he seized on a misplaced ball and prompted Tyler Roberts with a pinpoint pass which Roberts continued with a fine pass to the striker.

When Wolves resorted to blatant time wasting towards the close, the old soldier Pablo was the first to call them out on it resulting in referee Coote belatedly booking the worst offender, Neto. Then, in the final minute, only Ruy Patricio's superlative save from a Raphinha header prevented a fully deserved equalizer. Hernandez had set this up by suddenly switching the direction of attack with a clever chip wide to Ayling who then crossed for Raphinha.

Coming on as a substitute for Roberts against Aston Villa, Hernandez was belatedly greeted with a villainous aerial challenge from the crude full-back, Matt Targett. Jumping for an aerial ball from Diego Llorente, Pablo was sent crashing to the ground with a bang on the back of his head. Expecting that referee Peter Bankes would send the already booked Targett off, Pablo mimicked an elbow gesture, snarling "fuck off!" at the irresolute ref and was promptly booked for dissent.

Late in the match Pablo Hernandez cleverly smuggled the ball away from jostling midfielders and promptly found Harrison in space to deliver a cross which Raphinha ought to have converted.

Pablo Hernandez' final game for Leeds came in the last match of the season when fans were at long last back at Elland Road. Alongside Gaetano Berardi he received a special presentation from the club before kick-off. Berardi, the lionhearted defender sidelined for almost a year after a cruciate ligament injury, was warmly saluted by supporters. But it was the 36-year-old veteran, nicknamed 'El Mago' whom the crowd longed to see in action one last time. They sang his name throughout the match to the exhilarating tune of 'La Bamba', a unique example of a Spanish-language hit, first for Ritchie Valens in 1958 and then for Los Lobos in 1987.

Could Hernandez mark the occasion with a goal? Unfortunately not. He struck one fine effort which brought a brilliant save from West Bromwich keeper Sam Johnstone. Even so, Pablo's delicate right foot trap and instant pivot before he delivered his shot were in themselves a wonder to behold. And time after time he showed his football brain was as acute as ever when he provided passes for highly skilful teammates such as Rodrigo, Raphinha and Jack Harrison.

Had he still been on the pitch in the final 20 minutes when the Baggies conceded a penalty, this would of course have been an ideal opportunity for him to sign off with a goal. But by that time Pablo had departed with tears in his eyes and a permanent place in the hearts of all Leeds United supporters.

JUST CALL HIM CLICKY

MATEUSZ KLICH

Before Marcelo Bielsa arrived, Mateusz Klich's whole career had been one of disappointment and he was widely written off as one of Victor Orta's dodgy purchases. Then Bielsa totally transformed the bearded Pole with the high and tight haircut into a key member of the Leeds United team. Instead of being an outsider with an unpronounceable name he became a heroic figure under his new nickname 'Clicky.'

What was it that Bielsa saw in Klich, a man who'd been farmed out between Wolfsburg, Kaiserslautern, Zwolle and Twente and who contributed only the occasional goal? As well as that, Bielsa's predecessor, Thomas Christiansen, only picked Klich once, blamed him for slipping in possession leading to a goal by Cardiff City and virtually banished him thereafter.

We don't know the answer to that for certain since Klich made it clear in interviews that what was said between him and his manager must remain confidential. It may well be, however, that what commended him to Bielsa was his intelligence plus his excellent English. At the time Bielsa was struggling to make himself understood in English and he may have found it more comfortable to talk to someone else for whom English was a second language.

In interview Mateusz Klich was highly articulate about the satisfaction he got from playing football Bielsa-style. "I believe in possession-based attacking football" he said, adding "obviously there's a risk with that but we can play without fear of making mistakes." Alluding to Bielsa's insistence on a high standard of physical fitness, Klich revealed "I've never felt so good in my life –he saved my career and I only wish I'd met him 10 years earlier."

Elaborating on Bielsa's football philosophy Klich commented "Marcelo doesn't just want to win games, he also wants to dominate the ball and play good football. As for me, I don't want to run behind the ball and maybe get a point with a late penalty or something like that."

Nevertheless he indicated that there was a pragmatic side to Leeds' head coach. "In our first season back the aim is survival then after that we can build" he said. This clearly implied that Bielsa would show little interest in competitions such as the Carabao Cup and even the FA Cup, preferring to rest his key players in order to avoid potential injury in non-essential games.

In his two Championship seasons at Leeds under Bielsa, 2018-19 was the standout. That was when he scored 10 goals at a ratio of one every four and a half games. One of these was in the sensational clash with Aston Villa in April 2019 just before Bielsa ordered the team to let Villa score because they had a man down injured when Klich scored. Klich himself had been menacingly grabbed by Hourihane and Mings in the aftermath of that and was noncommittal in interview when asked about Bielsa's decision.

Mateusz Klich began his Premiership career in splendid style by scoring a brilliant goal against Liverpool which tied the score at 3-3. His Anfield goal was a triumph of ice cold despatch. True, he profited from sloppy play by van Dijk but the way he teed himself up and waited for a moment before blasting a half volley beyond Alisson was like a dagger to the heart of the Liverpool defence.

Klich didn't go on from strength to strength after Anfield. His subsequent shooting was wayward and he was at fault in opting to strike when too far out from goal. What's more, his defensive sloppiness was shown up at Old Trafford when he failed to track Scott McTominay for two goals in quick succession in the opening minutes.

Marcelo Bielsa's seemingly infinite patience with the faltering Pole finally came to an end after the wretched home defeat against Brighton when he was benched for the visit to St James Park. It was Rodrigo's early injury at the King Power Stadium which led to Klich's return. It seemed as if his demotion had proved a wake-up call because he played a prominent part in the defeat of Leicester City, not only switching play intelligently but putting himself about to the extent that he was booked for a ruthless challenge on Mendy which left the chubby little Frenchman howling in pain. Finally it was Klich who provided the penultimate pass for the third goal, picking out Bamford with a deftly delivered ball.

In March Mateusz Klich's season seemed curtailed after a positive Covid test. Yet Klich made a better-than-expected recovery and returned to the side for the final 10 minutes of the home game against Liverpool.

Against Spurs on the 8th May Mateusz Klich finally began to look like his old self, adding strength and strong running to his undoubted intelligence. The first man to spot this was an opponent, namely Hojberg who grabbed Clicky by the scruff of the neck as he started to speed past him. Before long Klich was launching a tiptop crossfield pass to Dallas who then embarrassed Aurier so badly he was lucky not to concede an own goal.

This was the day fans saw the real Klich re-emerge and he would have scored with a fierce swirling shot had not Lloris pulled off a world-class save. Keeping up his energy level to the final minutes

Klich linked with Koch and Raphinha to set up Rodrigo for the clinching third goal.

Against Burnley Mateusz Klich scored his first goal in open play since his excellent effort at Anfield on the opening day. He began the move deep in his own half swapping passes with Raphinha. He may well have intended to find Bamford who was barged down by the big- eared battering ram Tarkowsky in the centre circle. So Klich decided to go it alone till he reached the D where he fired a marvellous curling shot using Burnley defenders as shields and placing the ball just inside the post out of reach of the despairingly diving keeper Peacock- Farrell.

Before the end of the season Marcelo Bielsa gave Klich leave of absence for probable inclusion in the Polish squad for Euro 2021.

THE BARGAIN BUY

ROBIN KOCH

Robin Koch's Leeds career didn't get off to an auspicious beginning. For starters, he was clearly a second best choice for a new central defender in the eyes of both the fans and the manager. Ben White had been on season-long loan from Brighton and Hove Albion. White might have been a quietly spoken lad with a Dorset accent but he was an ever present at Elland Road, a tough tackler who was also a cultured distributor. In interview Ben expressed his gratitude to the supporters who, as he put it, "really took me to their hearts." Marcelo Bielsa rated White highly both as a player and a person and three successive bids were put in for him. '£18 million, are you having a laugh?, 22 million, you've got to be kidding?, 25 million? you can do miles better'– that appeared to be Brighton's attitude. All along the line the suspicion was that they seemed to be hanging back in hopes that Liverpool could be tempted to part with a king's ransom to sign a guy who, at only 22, had his whole football future ahead of him.

Fed up to the back teeth with England's inflated transfer market, Victor Orta looked elsewhere and recruited the German international Robin Koch from Freiburg for a mere £13 million.

Not only had Koch replaced a fan favourite who wanted to sign for Leeds but, on a lighter level, the mispronunciation of his surname caused either embarrassment or amusement all-round. On fansites the reactions differed. One lad revelled in phallic puns while another deliberately altered the pronunciation to 'Coach' while a third fansite guy-who knew that 'Koch' means 'Cook' in German ventured to suggest that the new recruit should be renamed as 'Robin Cook.' No one thought to ask the man himself how his surname should be pronounced. Koch spoke good English and seemed relatively relaxed but stereotypes about Germans lacking a sense of humour may have prevailed.

Robin Koch's debut at Anfield did not go well. For starters, he lacked an experienced central defensive partner. With Liam Cooper sidelined after injury on Scotland duty, the Dutchman Pascal Struijk deputised. But it was Koch not Struijk whose fallibility was soon exposed.

In the third minute Liverpool were awarded a dubious penalty after Mane danced round Dallas before pulling the ball back to Salah who promptly shot. The ball struck Koch on the knee and flew up to his outstretched right arm. Salah instantly appealed and referee Michael Oliver pointed to the spot while vice-captain Luke Ayling led the protests. Koch himself seemed phlegmatic, taken aback by Liverpool's fast-paced inter-passing.

Mo Salah, who hardly ever misses from the penalty spot, filled his lungs with air before banging the ball home. Sky pundit Jamie Carragher, Scouser to the core though he is, was sympathetic to Robin Koch– "that's 'arsh that, I feel for the lad!"

Despite Jack Harrison's superb equaliser, Leeds soon fell behind again. This time there was no mitigation for Robin Koch's blunder. Robertson easily outpaced Hernandez and, forcing a corner, he took it himself. Then Koch let Virgil van Dijk rush away from him, van Dijk hurled himself airborne and headed the ball powerfully home through the diving Meslier's gloves.

Sky's double act promptly kicked in as Jamie Carragher piped up– "ya berra get used to that, cock!" Martin Tyler hurriedly explained, in case viewers of a nervous disposition should be upset by the Scouser's language, "that's his name, by the way." Carra, undeterred, said "I've been waitin' twenty minutes to say that."

Carragher was lost in wonderment at the greatness of Mo Salah but a couple of minutes later Jamie's joy was cut short in an embarrassing exchange with Tyler. When Tyler noted that "Keita's stopped there by Koch", he pronounced the German surname in impeccably guttural tones. Carragher caught on–"is tharrow ya say it?" he wondered. Tyler retorted that "you've got to get a bit of a 'khggh' at the end of it, you see." Then he made a sniffy remark which the Scouser didn't dig for one moment. "That should come quite naturally to you, I would have thought." The guy from Bootle had heard enough over the years about his heavy accent, all the astute analysis he'd done week after week on Monday Night Football and they were still going on about it; he rightly refused to take the bait from the septuagenarian Cestrian.

As the weeks passed Robin Koch got more and more used to the hurly-burly of the Premiership. He didn't turn out to be the latest incarnation of Franz Beckenbauer but, at 13 million quid, fans began to see him as a bargain and noted his sorties into midfield to take part in constructive movements. But just as it all seemed to be going right it went wrong again.

After only seven minutes at Stamford Bridge facing Chelsea, Koch went down grimacing in pain at a corner. He had to hobble off. So Diego Llorente, short of match fitness, made his long-delayed Leeds debut. Sadly Llorente would be injured himself before the end of the game and it would be six weeks before he was fit enough to return.

For Koch the prognosis was worse. He was diagnosed with a torn meniscus and it would be at least three months before he'd be available again.

With Liam Cooper intermittently sidelined, this was the signal for pundits to spin their narrative about Leeds' allegedly incorrigible vulnerability from set pieces. Koch's injury was rarely if ever referred to while Diego Llorente was treated as a non-person and never even mentioned. In actual fact the problem was that makeshift centre backs such as Liam Ayling simply lacked –despite their valiant efforts –the necessary height to outjump tall forwards intent on gobbling up free kicks and corners.

Robin Koch's full recovery from injury was signalled at the Etihad when he came on for a full half hour. More than just an extra body in the defensive wall, he was too clever for Sterling just as he had been in the reverse fixture, tracking the England international back and dispossessing him just as he shaped to shoot.

Robin Koch had by far his best game for Leeds when they faced Spurs at Elland Road. With Kalvin Phillips not yet sufficiently recovered from injury to come off the bench till the final minute, he deputised for the linchpin in defensive midfield. Playing the part as to the manner born, Koch confidently cleared a short corner in the opening minutes.

The German played a prominent part when the Whites took the lead in the 13th minute. Noting that Aurier was too slack to mark Harrison, he advanced menacingly and promptly fed Harrison whose cross led to Dallases' goal.

In contrast to the blithering Tyler Roberts, Koch was coolness personified as he robbed Son and passed to Dallas before Roberts' misplaced pass spoiled a good opportunity.

Yet to score for the Whites, Koch was distinctly unlucky when he blasted a fierce 25 yard drive which was all set to fly past Lloris before a flukey deflection off Hojberg sent it narrowly wide. Koch's next contribution was his elegant pass inside Hojberg to Klich and in truth the German was striding around Elland Road like an absolute commander. Ruthless as well as intelligent, he was booked for clipping Son's ankles as the South Korean sought to set up a break.

Koch continued in imperious style with cleverly executed passes. And he was showing himself a complete teammate, quick to congratulate Illan Meslier after his marvellous save from Aurier's deflected shot. At the very end after his pre-assist for Rodrigo's goal he raced forward and exuberantly hugged both the scorer and the assister, Raphinha.

Before the season ended Marcelo Bielsa gave Koch leave of absence to prepare for probable inclusion in the German squad for Euro 2021.

FROM ZERO TO HERO

DIEGO LLORENTE

O pinion was divided as to whether Victor Orta had pulled off a major coup or been sold a pup when in September 2020 he forked out €21 million to cash-strapped Real Sociedad for the signature of Spanish international centre back Diego Llorente. There was no doubt that Llorente was a cultured central defender with a remarkably accurate passing range and also able to subdue the best opponents with perfectly timed tackles. He'd proved this against Ronaldo in more than one clash between Spain and Portugal.

The other side of the coin was Llorente's proneness to injury. Born in Madrid, he naturally aspired to play for Real but had been discarded as an 18-year-old for that very reason. Six years later, while starring with Real Sociedad, he was operated on for a distal fracture of the left fibula with the insertion of a screwed plate. Simultaneously undergoing an ankle arthroscopy, he made a very satisfactory recovery. Still, in Spain, eyebrows were raised at the prospect of Llorente becoming immersed in the rugged hurly-burly of the Premiership not to mention enduring the ultra-intensive conditioning which Marcelo Bielsa insisted on. Spanish sceptics foresaw a spate of muscular injuries.

Llorente, an intelligent man who'd taken the trouble to learn basic English, was well aware of the risks. It would have been far easier to have stayed where he was, relaxing on the sun-soaked beaches of San Sebastian alongside his beautiful wife, the former Ana Lopez. Still, he'd set his mind on taking his game to a further level under the coaching of Bielsa whose reputation in Spain remained without peer.

The sceptics were smirking when, following an injury sustained on international duty, Llorente's Leeds debut was delayed for over two months. It took place in inauspicious circumstances against Chelsea at Stamford Bridge on December 5. Short of match fitness, he was actually on the subs' bench expected to do no more than make a brief appearance late in the game if circumstances permitted. But in actual fact he was on the field in the eighth minute after a serious injury to Robin Koch.

It was one of the very few games in the season where limited crowd attendance was permitted. Following Boris Johnson's temporary relaxation of restrictions, Chelsea were permitted to have 2000 supporters present. Bielsa had rightly objected –but in vain –to the total ban on even a bare minimum of Leeds' fans.

After the Whites had taken an early lead with an excellent goal from Bamford following Phillips' brilliant pass, Chelsea soon equalized due to a mixup in the Leeds' defence. Though Diego Llorente had correctly moved up to play French striker Olivier Giroud offside, Luke Ayling had failed to follow suit and the big Frenchman was clear to thump the ball home.

On the other hand, Liam Cooper was a stalwart in defence and, encouraged by this, Diego Llorente started to move upfield making good use of the ball.

A bad mistake by Llorente looking to play out from defence under pressure presented the ball to the brilliant American Pulisic standing unmarked in the D. Thankfully he failed to control it and Cooper quickly cleared the danger.

While Cooper and Llorente were establishing a good partnership from scratch, Cooper had the much-vaunted German Timo Werner in his pocket and when, just before half-time, Pulisic burst forward dangerously, Llorente stopped him with an excellent sliding tackle.

In the second half, things took a different turn. Blues' keeper Mendy tried to find Giroud with a long kick. Llorente, going up for the header, found himself flattened by the rugged Frenchman. Some in the Stamford Bridge crowd claimed that the Leeds' central defender shrieked as he hit the deck. "Looks like a big fackin' stork, dasn'e, eh!", came a catcall.

From that moment on Llorente became the target of the moronic element in the Chelsea fanbase. There was more than half-an-hour of the match left but whenever he was on the ball –which was frequently–there were not just boos and catcalls but weird high-pitched noises like a pack of demented hyenas.

Sky should have been immediately calling out this cretinous nonsense but instead old Martin Tyler laughingly reminiscenced about the fierce rivalry between the two clubs in the 70s. To his credit, Llorente kept his cool under ridiculous provocation. Hoping for him to blunder, the mob had to be content with ref Kevin Friend booking him after a tactical foul on the Croatian Kovacic.

While Llorente had heard all about the Premiership rough-and-tumble, he experienced it in person at the time of Chelsea's second goal, having been ruggedly barged aside –as was Liam Cooper–by the ruthlessly physical Giroud before the burly Zouma headed in from a corner.

In the last minute of stoppage time, after Leeds had done their level best to secure an equalizer, Chelsea added a third when Llorente was outpaced by Pulisic who then scored after a pass from

Werner -having made a parallel run to the German in Chelsea's high-speed break.

After the match it transpired that Llorente had strained a muscle trying to keep pace with the American. He would not be fit to return to the fray until the new year.

It was January 26 against Newcastle at St James Park when Llorente finally reappeared. He lasted barely 10 minutes before going down with a pulled hamstring and needing to be replaced by Pascal Struijk. He seemed to be on the verge of tears as he hobbled to the touchline where Marcelo Bielsa placed a fatherly arm around him.

For six weeks after that Llorente was battling depression and receiving counselling from Bielsa while certain media elements mischievously invited Leeds fans to vote on whether he was "just desperately unlucky" or "made of glass."

The stakes were very high indeed when Diego Llorente returned against Southampton on February 23. Were he to succumb to another injury the club might have been obliged, albeit reluctantly, to come to a critical decision about his future. Mercifully, fortune smiled on him and from that moment on his true value became increasingly clear as game succeeded game.

Llorente was plainly off the pace at the start and prone to give the ball away; fortunately nothing came of his early errors. On the other hand, there were glimpses of Llorente's distributive skill such as when he found Dallas with a 30 yard crossfield ball but unfortunately Dallas was tackled out before he could make anything of it.

Leeds came close to scoring when Llorente cleverly drifted wide and Raphinha found him with a crafty pass which the Spaniard headed powerfully downward into the goalmouth where Cooper prodded the ball goalwards forcing McCarthy into a tip over.

Just turned the half hour there was an an extraordinary incident centering on Llorente and comprising a bad refereeing error from Andre Marriner, a hiatus of protest from Leeds, a reference to Stockley Park and VAR guiding Mr Marriner to reverse his decision.

Here's how it happened. James Ward-Prowse nutmegged Raphinha and found Nathan Tella, an Arsenal reject eager to make a good impression at a new club, who, with Ayling out of position, was unmarked down the left. Llorente came over to cover and Tella, finding the experienced international not falling for his simple stepover, went down in the box. Ward Prowse, son of a barrister and supremely confident, bellowed in Mr Marriner's ear and the ref pointed instantly to the spot.

Llorente was rightly indignant and protested at once, though hampered by his limited knowledge of English. "Not me, not me!" he snapped but he was obliged to resort to a gesture to indicate Tella's treachery. What it boiled down to, as would clearly be revealed by half-time video analysis, was that Tella jammed his knee into Llorente's shin and promptly went to ground. Ayling and Meslier had a clear view of it and raised their arms at once. When they'd had a word with Liam Cooper, he took the case up with Mr Marriner. Hitherto the stubborn Brummie had fixed the Spanish newbie with his glaring eyeballs but now Kevin Friend was in his ear from Stockley Park suggesting a rethink. The whistler jogged over to the monitor and promptly cancelled the penalty. Diego Llorente merely spread his arms in a 'WTF is all this nonsense about anyway' gesture.

As half-time approached, the match was packed with incident, some of it blatantly obvious some of it subtle. Llorente was dispossessed by Tella and only his wayward ball-- which Ayling cleared- prevented a probable goal; Llorente was furious with himself, punching his palm in vexation.

Shortly afterwards Llorente moved into midfield to intercept a pass from Adams meant for Armstrong; he boldly took a risk kicking the ball all the way back to Meslier- no danger was threatening but if he'd got it wrong he'd have plunged the side into trouble. Next thing he was deep in defence unhesitatingly slide tackling the advancing Armstrong to concede a corner from which nothing came. Slowly but surely Llorente was regaining his confidence and the benefit from that would be seen in the second half.

Scarcely had the second period begun when Bamford cleverly scored. He'd been fed with a fine pass from Roberts but it had been Diego Llorente whose immaculate pass to the Welshman had set up a devastating move.

On the hour came a fine Leeds move which might well have brought a goal; Llorente intercepted Salisu's pass, moved forward and played a good ball to Bamford; Bamford square passed to Alioski, Alioski played a really good ball to Raphinha just wide of the 6 yard box and he found Llorente whose instant shot was reflex-kicked away by McCarthy. It was a shame the Spaniard didn't score on his return but he was contributing a lot just the same, not merely surviving.

Three days later Leeds faced Aston Villa at home and the heavily physical Villa were benefiting from the indulgence of rookie ref Peter Bankes. Llorente was charged with marking Ollie Watkins, a striker trumpeted by the media and already capped by Southgate.

Before long Mr Bankes tok no notice when, tussling for the ball with Watkins, Llorente angrily gestured that the Villan had been pulling his shirt.

Just before half-time there was a further incident involving Watkins and Llorente. Tripped by the Torquay man, Llorente fell, clutching his shin and rolling about in anguish; when Watkins hauled him to his feet by his shirt, Llorente was furious; Luke Ayling protested to Mr Bankes while Cooper, Struijk and Meslier verbally warned Watkins to cut the crap.

Sky made sarcastic remarks about the contrast between Llorente's apparent agony one moment then jumping up the next. They incorrectly said that Llorente was squaring up yet he'd done nothing of the kind, his protests were purely verbal. The unspoken implication, with more than a hint of xenophobia, was of course that Llorente was shamming, but far more likely, the Spanish centre back, only just emerging from a run of injuries, feared he'd sustained another-this time deliberately inflicted by Watkins; when Watkins dragged him to his feet, however, pain gave way to anger. Sky praised Mr Bankes for admonishing Watkins but in actual fact he should have booked him.

Five minutes into the second half there was a further tussle for the ball between Watkins and Llorente; Watkins backed in but finding Llorente too clever for him, he brought the Spaniard down- once again Mr Bankes should have produced the yellow card but failed to do so.

This was the Premiership hurly-burly all right and Diego Llorente knew he had to adjust to it.

By this time Llorente had established friendly rapport with Luke Ayling after Luke sought his advice on long passing from defence. The pair of them combined to protest a penalty award in the London Stadium against West Ham.

Lingard duly converted the penalty but Diego Llorente was coping well with Michail Antonio, confident that his superior skill would win out against the burly Londoner, a prolific striker built like the Olympic sprinters who formerly competed in this stadium. But Leeds were undone a second time when Cresswell forced a corner off Ayling. Antonio pinned Meslier and neither Ayling nor Llorente could prevent the scrapper centre back Dawson charging in to head the ball home. This was rank bad defence, no question about it.

Early in the second half Diego Llorente was deprived of what would have been his first Premiership assist. He was aghast when Patrick Bamford's radar was for once off kilter after Llorente's superb slide rule pass-stabbed all of twenty yards and perfectly bisecting Dawson and Diop-had played the centre forward clean through.

Early on in the home game against Chelsea there was a bizarre incident involving Luke Ayling and Diego Llorente. Attempting a rushed clearance, Ayling could only lash the ball against Llorente's chest whence it rebounded over Meslier's head to roll back off the back of the crossbar safely into the keeper's gloves. There might have been a very different outcome of course and Luke apologized to Diego with a friendly tap on the back of the Spaniard's head.

Afterwards Llorente was in commanding form shutting out the German attacking midfielder Kai Havertz and, when Timo Werner emerged as a substitute, similarly subduing him.

A rare error of judgement by Phillips at the start of the second half seemed to let Havertz in yet Diego Llorente's last-ditch tackle put the German clean off his shot enabling Meslier to save.

At the end of the day in a match where the pundits had been salivating about a probable goalfest, it ended up as a goalless draw; in fact it was a considerable achievement for Leeds to have stymied the normally free-flowing Chelsea but there was insufficient emphasis on the improvement in the Whites' defence and Diego Llorente, in particular, passed under the media radar. His central defensive partnership with Pascal Struijk looked the most secure Leeds had fielded -with the elegant Llorente marshalling play and the sturdily built Struijk unobtrusively in the right place at the right time.

Early doors away to Fulham Llorente delivered an excellent long ball, all of 35 yards bouncing into Bamford's path with Joachim Anderson quickly embarrassed. After Bamford unselfishly heeded a call from Tyler Roberts, Bamford felt the need to offer an explanation to Llorente and, nodding in Roberts' direction, said "I heard him shout!"

In first half stoppage time Llorente was within inches of getting on the end of a superb Raphinha freekick which had eluded the entire Fulham defence. As he watched the ball bounce down into no man's land just beyond his outstretched bootstuds, Llorente could only grasp empty air in despair at what would have been his first Leeds goal.

In the second half Llorente easily trapped a wild Fulham clearance and found Harrison with a perfect 30 yard pass. Jack jinked past Anguissa and Ola Aina and went on to shoot from an angle only for Areola to save his shot.

Leeds had prevailed against a fiercely physical Fulham indulged by a lenient referee. But one of the most significant moments in the match was Patrick Bamford's effective apology to Diego Llorente for having backheeled his excellent pass to a clamorous Tyler Roberts. That very fact in itself established how far Diego Llorente had come in a matter of weeks from an almost forgotten teammate consigned to the treatment room to a figure of real authority within the side.

Resuming after the international break which saw him performing solidly for Spain, Diego Llorente showed his value to Leeds in the home game against Sheffield United. The Whites held a 2-1 lead yet, despite rocking the Blades with a series of sweeping counter-attacks, they might well have been pegged back albeit undeservedly from a freekick. It was Llorente who saved the day with a stupendous defensive header executed while off-balance running towards his own goal! In addition, he compensated for a dangerously careless pass by Raphinha with a formidable sliding tackle-before giving Raphinha a helluva rollocking!

While Stuart Dallases' two goals were what won the away match against Manchester City, it was Diego Llorente's splendid defensive display which, more than anything else, ensured that the ten men didn't lose. He was the one who marshalled the defence, leading by example in the team's hour of need. Time and again he calmly cleared the danger; Raheem Stirling could do nothing against him and his vertical takeoff header-when Jesus looked odds on to convert Fernandinho's cunningly flighted chip-was a wonder to behold.

Diego Llorente was not at his best in the first half of the home game against Liverpool.

Having never before faced a side playing with Liverpool's unrelenting speed, Llorente seemed transformed as the Reds started to look tired early in the second half. When he dispossessed Mane with consummate ease and sent Alioski flying down the flank with a first class crossfield ball, it signalled the turning point in the game.

Diego Llorente and Pascal Struijk looked more and more a splendid central defensive partnership with Llorente's skill and excellent distribution complemented by Struijk's physical ruggedness and fine positional sense.

When Juergen Klopp belatedly introduced Premiership top scorer Mo Salah, Llorente faced his most dangerous opponent of the season. Yet when Thiago's marvellous lofted 35 yard pass seemed to send Salah clean away, it was Llorente who stayed with him, forcing the Egyptian to shoot earlier than he wanted, ending up a yard off target.

The climax of Llorente's display came when he scored the equalising goal, his first for Leeds, with only four minutes left on the clock. Struijk had narrowly failed to get on the end of Harrison's inswinging corner yet Llorente, jumping high, bravely got his napper between those of Kabak and Firmino and he aimed his downward header beyond the stranded Alisson.

He celebrated uninhibitedly, leaping up and pointing skywards. This was no contrived pseudo-religious gesture because, as he revealed afterwards in his improving English, he was dedicating his goal to his beloved grandpa who passed on only six weeks before. Llorente was engulfed by his jubilant teammates shouting his nickname –'Diggy.'

It almost seemed as if Llorente's fine performance might have ended unhappily when, in the very last minute, he dispossessed Salah with an impeccable sliding tackle. When Salah' momentum led to him treading on Llorente's shin, it looked inadvertent even though it was checked and cleared by VAR. Llorente had no problem with Salah but he gripped his leg anxiously only to resume hobbling after treatment. Happily he was running normally as the match finished.

When Manchester United came to Elland Road, it soon became clear they hoped to trouble Leeds with long balls. Victor Lindelof hit a really good one in the opening minutes and Diego Llorente was caught out. But Marcus Rashford let the ball run away from him and had to move wide right. That gave Llorente a chance to adjust his possession and Rashford shot wastefully wide. After that Llorente's display was impeccable.

Danger loomed again when another high ball saw Rashford getting beyond Ayling but Llorente promptly moved in to make a vital sliding interception. Llorente's partnership with Pascal Struijk proved a barrier which United could not penetrate and, even though Lindelof caught Ayling out in the closing stages with a surprise long ball, there was Llorente striding imperturbably to the rescue.

Diego Llorente had transformed Leeds' defence in the second half of the season. For months he'd been little more than an introverted outsider almost always in the treatment room. But, as soon as he'd returned to full fitness, he'd become a heroic figure greatly valued by his teammates. Though he never modified his old style haircut, he made great progress learning English and becoming completely integrated. His adventures with Leeds United didn't go unnoticed in his homeland and he was selected to join the Spanish squad for Euro 2021.

STANDING TALL -IN MORE
WAYS THAN ONE

ILLAN MESLIER

When a lad named Illan Meslier arrived unknown at Elland Road, he was rumoured to be a splendid piece of scouting. The young French goalkeeper had been signed from Breton club Lorient and, speaking little English at the time, was helped to settle in by Patrick Bamford who spoke his language fluently.

Meslier got his chance following the FA's punishment of veteran keeper Kiko Casilla, formerly third choice with Real Madrid. Casilla was convicted of racially abusing a Charlton Athletic player and suspended for eight weeks. Barely twenty but standing fully two metres tall, Meslier never looked back and kept seven clean sheets in ten games. Though he had the face of a boy, his contrastingly deep voice reminded fans of Darth Vader.They heard it in interviews which indicated he was making rapid progress in English. He answered questions with a disarming smile, thought carefully about his replies and radiated confidence.

His Premiership debut came at Anfield where, though Leeds conceded four goals, none of them were his fault. Indeed it might have been even worse had he not leaped up to push a looping ball over the bar when it looked as if it would drop just under it. Had that happened it would have been an own goal by fellow debutant Pascal Struijk. Seeing the blood drain from the Dutchman's face, Meslier gave him a mock -reproachful grin and Struijk recovered to acquit himself well.

Meslier's breakthrough match came at Bramall Lane where he almost single-handedly defied Sheffield United in a hardfought Yorkshire derby. Clearly he was a totally unknown quantity to the Blades who at kick off were heard muttering "who the fuck's this lad in goal?" They soon found out.

When a nifty backheel from McBurney put Lundstram in one-on-one against Illan from 12 yards, the stocky Scouser gave it all he'd got. Raising his fist to claim what he thought would be a certain goal, he stood open mouthed as Meslier brought off a phenomenal save. In an instant he shifted his weight from left to right and dived at full stretch to punch the ball behind for a corner from which nothing came. His second great stop came when he defied the Irishman Stevens who seized on a mistake by Klich and sprinted past first Dallas then Harrison. "Gotcha this time!" yelled the Blade as he shot but he was wrong. Meslier jumped to his full height and coolly palmed the ball over the bar. Though Bamford made victory secure with a late goal it was Meslier who almost single-handedly ensured that the Whites would not lose.

When Manchester City came to Elland Road, Kevin de Bruyne crashed a colossal swerving freekick against Meslier's near post with the game only three minutes old. Meslier had desperately adjusted his weight but had been beaten to the wide. The Belgian was of course a world-class star who could make anybody look a fool but Sky's Martin Tyler chose to dwell on Meslier's youthful appearance, seeming to imply that Leeds were foolish to rely on someone so lacking in worldly wisdom. Little did Tyler know that had Illan not opted for a football career, he would have been starting a university course in France. Meslier made no more mistakes against City's vaunted attack and Leeds gained a draw.

Next when the Whites were humbled by the cleverly interpassing Leicester City, Meslier slipped up fumbling Jamie Vardy's diving header and the ball ran loose to Tielemans for a tap In. Yet he was blameless for Leicester's other three goals.

At Selhurst Park when Leeds suffered another heavy defeat, Meslier was criticised by pundits for being beaten at his near post yet he was the victim of a freak deflection, one so bizarre as to leave him blinking in disbelief.

At home to Arsenal, Leeds had outplayed the Gunners but it looked as if they'd sneak an undeserved last-minute win with a breakaway when Saka was too quick for Dallas and too nimble for Cooper. But it was Meslier who denied them showing great presence of mind as well as truly gymnastic agility. Firstly he disoriented Saka by calmly biding his time and making the Arsenal forward drift wide. One minute Meslier was down on his knees, the next he was stretching out a gloved fist to beat the ball away for a corner which yielded nothing despite the fact that he was given scant protection by referee Anthony Taylor when harassed-as he had been throughout the game- by the away side.

Against Burnley Meslier was implicitly branded a villain by Sean Dyche's stentorian bawling when he flattened Ben Mee with an accidental knee in the back. The real culprit was of course the inexperienced referee Robert Jones who should have awarded the home side a penalty. Meslier seemed blithely unconcerned by the controversy.

During the course of the match animosity developed between two fiery characters – Gjanni Alioski and Ashley

Barnes. The pair of them were exchanging angry verbals with the clear potential of a sending off. When Mr Jones was looking the other way, Meslier placed a gentle restraining arm on Alioski's shoulder before roughly barging Barnes. Then in the last minute he saved a point for his side when he leaped up to a high inswinging corner and punched the ball over the bar. His teammates rushed to hug him in collective appreciation of the way in which he'd stood tall –not just physically but psychologically!

Unquestionably he had a bad day in the Tottenham Hotspur stadium when he was chiefly responsible for two of Spurs' three goals. His first error resulted in a penalty after the careless pass out which put Harry Winks in possession. Winks played in Bergwijn whom Alioski promptly tripped in the box. Later Meslier fell across Alderweireld's innocuous header from a corner. The ball bounced off his belly and rolled over the goal-line before he could scoop it out.

At the final whistle he was consoled by his compatriot Hugo Lloris, not merely out of sentiment but because Lloris knew full well from the French media just how well Illan Meslier had been doing in previous matches. The Spurs keeper's demeanour clearly showed that he recognised Meslier, fourteen years his junior, as his heir apparent in the French national team.

In the postmatch interview Marcelo Bielsa stoutly defended Meslier, pointing out his many excellent saves in previous games.

At St James's Park against Newcastle he showed raw courage after Ryan Fraser's cunningly flighted far post cross had confused both Struijk and Alioski. Jacob Murphy, racing in regardless, knocked him over with an accidental knee to the head which left Illan lying face down on the turf. He looked groggy as the physios raced to his assistance but, when he alertly reassured them during the concussion test, they okayed him to resume and with an imperturbable shrug he did just that. Even better, he pulled off a point-blank reflex save when a bullet header from Shelvey looked certain to grab the Geordies an equaliser.

Meslier's worst game for Leeds came in the 4-2 defeat at the Emirates. He was wholly or partly to blame for three of Arsenal's goals, twice allowing himself to be beaten at the near post and, worst of all, dwelling on the ball when there was no danger. This effectively invited Bukayo Saka to challenge him before he clipped the England international's ankles thus conceding a totally gratuitous penalty. While Sky pundit Jimmy Hasselbaink reminded viewers of Meslier's excellent saves earlier in the season, it seemed to Leeds' fans vital for the 20-year-old shot stopper to quit farting about in situations such as these and to concentrate on clearing his lines.

When Illan reappeared, at the Molyneux Stadium five days later it was obvious Marcelo Bielsa had been on his case and had referred him to the goalkeeping coach, Marcos Abad. For starters he looked different, kitted out in a blue and black jersey instead of the wan orange of the Emirates. He was soon getting briskly on with the job, kicking long and punching powerfully to rebuff Wolves' aerial attacks. What's more, he leaped full stretch to deny Neto with a fine one-handed save.

His sole reward was to be a slice of grotesque bad luck. No keeper would have stood a chance against Adama Traiore's ferocious accelerating drive but, when the ball rebounded from the junction of bar and post, it struck Illan Meslier on the back as he lay grounded after his desperate attempt to save. From there it bounced gently into the net. Meslier was of course blameless in what was a freak incident yet he had to be debited with an own goal.

Meslier had relatively little to do in the home game against Aston Villa. He was blameless for El Ghazi's winner scored after only five minutes when he was left at the mercy of the Dutch winger by Helder Costa's dreadfully slow reaction to danger.

Later in the match Illan, pissed off by Peter Bankes' timid refereeing, strode out to confront Villan Ollie Watkins who, nonplussed by Diego Llorente's composure on the ball, was looking to bully the skilful Spaniard and had sent him sprawling with a kick on the shin. Towering over Watkins, Meslier warned him to cut the crap.

Against Chelsea Lady Luck made it up to Illan Meslier for the cruel trick she played on him against Wolves. This time when Ayling's attempted clearance rebounded off Llorente over the keeper's head, he was relieved to see it roll down off the back of the crossbar and drop gently into his gloves.

Against Fulham only an absolutely fantastic save by Illan Meslier prevented the Cottagers' grabbing the lead against the run of play; Fulham's Nigerian striker Josh Maja fairly belted the ball at him from point blank range yet Meslier didn't merely parry the strike with the obvious danger of a follow-up but with wrists of steel he turned it several yards away for Ayling to blast a clearance.

Illan Meslier faced his sternest test of the season when Leeds went down to ten men in the second half at the Etihad. He rose to the occasion splendidly, maturing minute by minute as a sweeper-keeper alertly reading danger and clearing impeccably. And, not to be forgotten, it was his pass to Helder Costa in stoppage time which began the move leading to Dallas' winner.

For most of the first half against Liverpool at Elland Road, Meslier had been rarely troubled despite Liverpool's dominance of possession. With only 10 minutes remaining in the match, however, he nearly sunk his own side by a dreadful mistake. His intermittent weakness of passing out poorly with short balls resurfaced when he gave it away to Salah of all people. Fortunately the Egyptian was unusually slow to react and his delayed shot was blocked off Struijk for a corner.

Meslier looked horrified by his blunder, contorting his face and muttering before raising a hand in apology to his teammates. Still shaken up, he ran out at the corner but failed to claim the ball.

Jota's looping header seemed goalbound even though Harrison had raced back to stand on the line. To his great credit, Meslier got his bearings back and made full use of his two metres frame to punch the ball off the top of Firmino's head and over the bar. Completely undaunted, he shouted "come on!!" in his menacing deep voice thus reassuring every man in a white shirt that the danger was over and they must press on.

So good was Leeds' defence against United at Elland Road that Illan Meslier was almost unemployed till a minute before half-time. Then a rare error from Struijk- a mistimed tackle on Dan James- conceded a free kick more than 25 yards out. Marcus Rashford delivered a tremendous drifting, dipping, speeding-up shot which seemed bound for the back of the net. Yet Meslier, though he saw the ball late, hurled himself into the air and with a mighty one-handed shove sent it high, wide and clear.

The young keeper didn't lose his concentration after his phenomenal save. He remained totally unflappable at the corner calling on his teammates to "come on!" Even though Maguire managed to break free, he failed to keep his header down.

Interviewed the day after the match, Illan was asked whether he knew he'd become the youngest Premiership goalie to keep ten clean sheets in a season. He replied that he'd been told about it after the match. The interviewer joked that he'd now be asking for a pay rise. Meslier was lost for a moment by the use of idiomatic English but caught on quick that it meant a new contract. He laughed.

Illan Meslier played a vital part in Leeds' home game against Spurs. Having to watch his compatriot Hugo Lloris thwart his teammates with world-class saves, he answered with one of his own when, in the real mark of a top class keeper hitherto virtually unemployed, he pulled off a truly great save leaping at full stretch to foil a ferocious cross shot from Aurier which had taken a deflection off Alioski. Later he brilliantly saved a viciously angled shot from Lamela with his feet.

Meslier had little to do in the first half against Burnley at Turf Moor. But when Burnley began throwing their weight about early in the second and Vydra got past Struijk to fire a low angled shot, Meslier improvised a brilliant save going down and using his left leg to lever the ball behind for a corner which was cleared.

Later, when the Icelander Gudmondsson cleverly prompted Rodriguez into a deceptively difficult shot, Meslier again rescued Leeds with a sitting save. It may have had an element of luck about it as the ball rebounded from the Frenchman's thigh for a quickly cleared corner. But it was vital nevertheless.

Illan Meslier, the youngest goalie to keep ten Premiership clean sheets, had every right to feel deeply disappointed when he was excluded from the French squad for Euro 2021. His standing with Leeds' fans remained high and he was voted Young Player of the Season.

THE LINCHPIN

KALVIN PHILLIPS

For a couple of years after he first became fairly famous, Kalvin Phillips answered serious interview questions thoughtfully and nerdy ones lightheartedly. It was only when the Times got on his case in November 2020 that he opted to disclose that his father had been in jail for much of Kalvin's childhood and youth. Indeed Mark Phillips was currently incarcerated at Wealstun prison, ironically close to the Leeds United training ground at Thorp Arch. Kalvin had emerged from a mixed race Leeds family, his father born in Jamaica, his mum a girl of Irish heritage.

It was Lindsay Crosby who sacrificed herself to bring up a family of five on her own. Kalvin himself was a triplet but tragedy struck when Lacreesha, one of the other two, both girls, died at an early age. It was a tribute to his mother's dedication and to his own innate strength of character that he grew up a levelheaded lad. With his only father figure his beloved maternal grandad, he devoted himself to football at an early age. Indeed Kalvin was the last of a long line of gifted British street footballers. Living just above the poverty line in inner city Armley, on free school meals and with no money for computer games, he and his brother Terrell played out night after night kicking a ball about with a couple of other poor boys and, in his case, honing splendid soccer skills. Meanwhile his surviving siblings, responding to their mother's firmly instilled values, all turned out well with one sister going on to work in the prison service. One more figure completed the family circle. This was Kalvin's maternal grandmother, Val Crosby. A devoted Leeds supporter since way back when, Grannie Val featured in the documentary 'Take Us Home.' A warm-hearted lady, she loved her grandson and cherished him as he made rapid progress at Elland Road.

Fascinated with Leeds United and well versed in the club's history, Kalvin studied videos of Billy Bremner whose combination of high skill with ruthless resolution appealed to him. As a boy of 14, he saw the controversial film 'The Dammed United' and discussed its accuracy – or otherwise –with his grandad.

Given his chance at Elland Road by Neil Redfearn, ignored by Steve Evans but brought back into the fold by Garry Monk, Phillips became a more than useful attacking midfielder who could weigh in with goals every half a dozen games. Potentially he was far more than that but it took the arrival of Marcelo Bielsa to discern this.

Analysing video footage of Phillips, Bielsa came to three specific conclusions about the 22-year-old. He could "transfer the ball to a better space than the one in which he found it, cover for the defenders when the full backs went into all-out attack and, if the side came under attack, he would position himself to repel it."

Bielsa moved Kalvin Phillips back into a role as a defensive midfielder capable of instigating attacks from a deep lying position. He became the linchpin of Bielsa's Leeds, a key cog in the machine which would eventually secure the club's long desired return to the Premiership.

After their narrow failure to achieve this in Bielsa's first reason, the manager was deeply moved when he saw Kalvin Phillips weeping uncontrollably in the depth of his disappointment. Not only did he hug him but he presented him with a special token of his admiration, a replica shirt of Bielsa's first Argentinian club, the red and black stripes of Newells Old Boys. A bond was established from that moment on and, at the end of their second season together, Leeds United returned to the Premiership.

Off the field Kalvin was modest and unassuming. His Mercedes wasn't embellished with flashy extras and his girlfriend was no egregious Wag but the make up artist Ashleigh Behan, a girl who looked elegant in casual clothes. As far as his teammates were concerned, he got on well with all of them, remarking that he saw Leeds United as a family.

Just as Marcelo Bielsa was preparing the side for the most difficult opening fixture imaginable, away at Anfield against a Liverpool who'd won the title by 18 clear points, came news of Phillips' selection for England. But what might have proved a daunting distraction didn't turn out that way.

One down in the third minute as a result of a highly controversial penalty, Leeds hit back quickly with a splendid goal instigated by Kalvin Phillips. He'd spotted something, namely that Liverpool's right back, Trent Alexander-Arnold, wasn't tightly marking Jack Harrison as he should have been. Promptly summoning the ball from Meslier, Phillips despatched a perfectly weighted 30 yard pass right into Harrison's path on the flank. The result was that Harrison flummoxed both Arnold and Joe Gomez with his outstanding ball skill before cracking a shot beyond the world's best keeper, Alisson. Marcelo Bielsa rightly took pride in what his two young protégés had achieved.

Striking back each time Liverpool went ahead in this wonderfully fluctuating game, Leeds came within inches of taking a 4-3 lead. After Firmino had lost possession to Jack Harrison, chased after him and brought him down, it was Kalvin Phillips who took the freekick. 35 yards out, he leaned confidently back, lofted the ball over the leaping wall and curled it adroitly, aiming for just inside the near post. Alisson, shocked by the speed of it, hurled himself full length and just failed to get his fingertips to it as it skimmed the upright. Phillips was left anguished by the proximity to a perfect dead ball strike.

When Phillips caught the eye in his England debut against Denmark, it signalled open season for crass punditry designed to cast doubt on Marcelo Bielsa's expertise. As Paul Merson saw it, the Argentinian was restricting Phillips by giving him a carefully designed role instead of letting him run free. Merson wouldn't have been surprised "if the lad got fed up with it and asked for a transfer." As for Dion Dublin, he brushed aside any defensive errors Phillips made for his club blaming Bielsa for giving him strict man marking instructions.

Matters came to a head when Leeds lost one nil to Wolves. On 70 minutes Raul Jimenez was bent on shooting from the D though Leeds' defenders were packing the box. His shot wasn't a good one, Meslier was poised to save it yet Phillips unaccountably intervened only succeeding in heading the ball into his own net.

The goal was credited to Jimenez but in reality it was an own goal by Phillips. Luke Ayling beat the turf in vexation while a scowling Meslier berated the culprit and Phillips was left looking a complete clown as he rearranged his dishevelled topknot.

On social media a number of Leeds' fans gave Phillips dog's abuse, claiming he'd had "a stinker." This was unfair, he actually contributed a lot to the game but what on earth caused that rush of blood to make him stage that pseudo-heroic header?

Phillips was an impressionable lad, unlike his club teammates who have come up the hard way, no problem while he was under the guidance of Marcelo Bielsa, the greatest coach in the world but a different story when he was under the aegis of the England manager, Gareth Southgate. Had Phillips started to believe the pundit publicity? Maybe, maybe not but at least the question was in the air.

Having injured his shoulder in the final minutes of the Wolves game, Phillips didn't play against Leicester and then against Crystal Palace. Given that Leeds lost both games by a 4-1 margin, it certainly seemed that he'd been badly missed.

Kalvin returned, newly bearded, against Arsenal and looked as if he meant business from the get go. Tackling hard, intercepting, firing off good passes, keeping the vaunted Gunners' striker Aubemayang at bay and booked for a ruthless stamp on Ceballos, he instigated the move which led to Raphinha striking the post. The game ended in a nil nil draw but it was one Leeds fully deserved to win and in which Kalvin Phillips had been at the heart of things.

Kalvin had established a good rapport with the Brazilian newcomer Raphinha, quick to spot his vast potential and encouraging him to shoot which Raphinha duly did against Everton in the strike which won the game. Afterwards veteran Scottish pundit Graeme Souness, with no nationalistic axe to grind, picked out Phillips for praise saying "I like the lad and one thing about him is that he leaves a foot in!"

But against Chelsea at Stamford Bridge it was Phillips' silken skills not his vigorous tackling which caught the eye. In a move which was even better than the one he'd executed at Anfield, he played Patrick Bamford in with a fantastic 20 yard pass delivered from the junction of the halfway line and the touchline. Delivered with side spin, it curled beyond Chelsea's burly centre back Zouma right into Patrick Bamford's path. Though Bamford finished with poise and aplomb, he owed the opportunity to Kalvin Phillips. Already dubbed the 'Yorkshire Pirlo' by internationally aware Leeds fans, this was exactly the kind of thing that epitomised the accolade.

Unhappily, the very lapse into tactical indiscipline which first showed up against Wolves manifested itself again in—of all matches—the clash at Old Trafford when Leeds succumbed to United 6-2. Though Klich had been the main one to blame for the two early United goals, Phillips had slipped up badly for two others. Instructed to mark the Mancs' Portuguese playmaker Bruno Fernandes, he left his post after Cooper had kicked air. Yet Luke Ayling was keeping Martial at bay before Phillips rushed over to render unwanted assistance. Ayling, his concentration disturbed, lost possession and the loose ball ran for Fernandes, now revelling in Phillips' absence, to slam it home. Worse was to follow when Phillips lost Lindelof at a corner leaving the Swede with an easy tap in to make the score four nil. He was removed at half time.

Thankfully Kalvin Phillips was his normal highly effective self in subsequent games and when, after accumulating five bookings, he was suspended for the match against Brighton, Leeds looked markedly weaker in his absence.

A home against Crystal Palace he followed Marcelo Bielsa's instructions to the letter, not giving the Ghanaian striker Jordan Ayew a moment's peace or half a yard distance. His close marking was key to Leeds' victory and, with a brilliant interception plus pass, he instigated the move which led to the second goal. Sadly he sustained a calf injury in the closing minutes and was obliged to miss the game at the Emirates where Arsenal took full advantage of his absence accumulating a four nil lead by the opening minutes of the second half.

It was while recuperating from that injury that Kalvin was devastated to learn of the demise of his beloved Granny Val to whom Stuart Dallas and Liam Cooper led tributes during and after the victory against Southampton by displaying a white Leeds shirt with her name inscribed on it.

Back in action in his hometown against Chelsea, Phillips showed he was both cunning and rugged when he hesitated as the high wind held the ball up before he blocked Ziyech's shot. He was in the midst of things from the getgo contributing plenty to Leeds' revitalised defence.

The same thing was true in London against Fulham. He ruled midfield, subduing the combative Camerounian Anguissa in the process. What's more, he was a key figure in the vital 27 seconds segment of play which led to Leeds' crucial winning goal after Adebola Lookman fluffed his shot at the other end. Pouncing after Lookman's blunder, he spied Bamford clear on the halfway line and found him with a brilliant pass.

Kalvin Phillips was in his element during the epic defeat of City on April 10. Pissed off by the ref's problematic decisions, he was careful to bear in mind Marcelo Bielsa's insistence that, whilst you must of course be fully involved in the contest, a referee should be treated with respect at all times. So when Bernardo Silva kicked him on the back of his leg, he politely pointed out to Mr Marriner that he'd failed to observe the incident. When John Stones was awarded an unjustified freekick, Phillips merely enquired "hey ref, what was that for?"

But by the time Stones threw him down just as he was about to instigate what could have been a decisive breakaway –and this cynical act went unpunished– Kalvin's patience was exhausted. Totally professional, he leapt to his feet at once and assisted Llorente in rebuffing Stones. Once the danger was cleared, he vented his true feelings and told Mr Marriner to "fuck off!" Then, doubtless bearing the words 'dissent' and 'foul language' in mind, he dropped his voice to mutter further comment, this time inaudible. As it happened, the Birmingham-born official kept his cards in his pockets.

The second half scrap with City saw Phillips in the thick of the fray, reading danger and registering tough but fair tackles; he had a fire in his belly which the boys in blue could never match. As he sent Raphinha clear with a superb 30 yard pass, only an impeccable Ederson sliding tackle on his fellow Brazilian deprived Phillips of a goal assist.

Kalvin Phillips had the game of his life when Manchester United came to Elland Road on April 25. He remembered only too well that, in the reverse fixture, he'd been substituted at half-time after failing to stick to Marcelo Bielsa's strict instructions to shadow United's Portuguese kingpin Bruno Fernandes.

Boosted by his coaches' faith in him, Kalvin set about the same task remorselessly. At first Fernandes scoffed at his proximity and tried some sneaky backchat. Yet Phillips shrugged it off with a couldn't-care-less grin.

Keeping Fernandes within his sights didn't mean that Phillips was oblivious of other threats. Far from it, when Fred was found by a Greenwood chip, it was Phillipses' excellent tackle on the Brazilian which snuffed out the danger.

Later Fernandes sought to take advantage of Craig Pawson's indulgence and went down whining that he'd been fouled by Phillips. United got a soft decision but the petulant Portuguese playmaker could only thump his freekick over the bar.

Fernandes was completely unsettled by Phillipses' rigorous interventions and lost the ball to his unrelenting marker who calmly prompted Stuart Dallas for a quick left foot shot which was saved. The longer the game went on the more Fernandes was disturbed by the way Phillips was shadowing him and, even when he momentarily got clear, he was uncharacteristically hesitant before shooting wide. The key to the whole match was the way in which Kalvin Phillips completely undermined Bruno Fernandes' usual arrogance.

It wasn't just Fernandes who was shaken out of his stride. In the 27th minute Phillips robbed McTominay and instigated an attack which ended only with a marginal offside decision against Alioski.

The scowling McTominay, probably pissed off about his reduced stature after he'd been the star of the show in the December encounter, was looking to throw his weight about. He barged down

Phillips, an incident which was checked by VAR without subsequent action.

Aware of his teammates at all times, Kalvin rescued Jack Harrison after he'd been dispossessed by Fred. Then he blocked off the Brazilian's intended short pass to McTominay before rattling the lanky Lancastrian with a powerful but perfectly fair tackle. McTominay doubtless hoped to dupe the ref but it seemed Mr Pawson had wised up even though he hesitated for a second thus precluding Phillips from moving off with the ball. Kalvin complained briefly then jogged on.

Later on Fernandes found Phillips breathing down his neck yet again. The Mancs' kingpin rushed into a premature shot, clipping it well wide and shook his head in disbelief.

Just turned the hour a superb 35 yard crossfield ball from Kalvin Phillips came close to producing a goal. He sent Helder Costa clear down the left flank and when Costa lashed a shot, Wan-Bissaka flicked out a foot and deflected the ball high onto the roof of the net with Henderson stranded.

With a quarter of an hour left Marcelo Bielsa sought to escape from the stalemate and brought Robin Koch on. Now Koch took Phillipses' place in defensive midfield allowing Kalvin to move forward in search of a winner. Though this didn't materialize, it demonstrated Bielsa's total faith in Phillips.

In truth Kalvin Phillips had produced a performance worthy of his boyhood idol, the great Billy Bremner below banners displaying Bremner's motto –"side before self."

In the post match interview Marcelo Bielsa made a telling distinction as he singled out Phillips for great praise. "It's difficult to be aggressive without being violent yet Kalvin did exactly that" he said.

Kalvin Phillips may have been put on his mettle in the game against Burnley at Turf Moor by virtue of Robin Koch's excellent performance as his deputy against Spurs. Regardless of this, Phillips was to the fore with tremendous contributions. Early on he picked out Struijk with an excellent free kick which the burly centre back narrowly failed to convert.

Then he simultaneously trapped a high looping ball and converted it into a volleyed cross landing perfectly for Harrison. Had it not been for a desperate looping deflection by former Leeds' player Charlie Taylor, Harrison's tantalising low cross would have found Raphinha perfectly placed to hammer home.

Responding in characteristically forthright manner to Luke Ayling's command to "stand up to 'em" Phillips countered Burnley's ruggedly physical approach with a heavy tackle which sent the Czech Vydra hurtling to the turf and earned him a booking.

Then Kalvin delivered an absolutely splendid 30 yard pass to Harrison wide left even as Rodrigo made up the ground in midfield prior to his brilliant second strike.

Kalvin Phillips had an excellent game against Southampton away albeit limited to 45 minutes. His perfectly executed sliding tackle on Che Adams, who was clean through on goal after being prompted by Saints' danger man Nathan Tella, found Adams belatedly flagged offside. It didn't matter –Phillips had set the tone at a time when, following the loosening of governmental restrictions, Southampton had 8000 supporters in the stadium bawling them on at the top of their lungs.

Surprisingly Kalvin Phillips didn't reappear on the resumption and it was understood he sustained a slight injury in the closing seconds of the first half. Pascal Struijk moved into defensive midfield as his replacement.

Against West Bromwich Albion on the final day of the season Kalvin Phillips' combative defence was needed throughout against the resentful Brummies still smarting from their five nil humiliation in the reverse fixture. Yet Phillips was favoured by fortune when a blunder from keeper Sam Johnstone allowed him to score his only Premiership goal of the season with a free kick.

The match ended unhappily for Kalvin, however, when in the last minute of normal time, his lapse of concentration let Robson-Kanu in to score. Then, clearly attempting to atone for his blunder, he launched a rugged tackle on the dangerous Diangana. Though he got the ball, he brought down the West Brom winger with his trailing leg. Diangana fell heavily on Phillipses' shoulder and Leeds' linchpin was clearly in severe pain. After two minutes treatment from the physios he got to his feet tentatively clutching his shoulder and grimacing. Mr Coote waited till then to produce a harsh yellow card after what was no more than a heavy challenge.

Happily the injury was not as bad as at first feared and Kalvin Phillips was cleared to join the England squad for Euro 2021.

THE BRAZILIAN REVELATION

RAPHINHA

Signed in the last hours of the transfer window, Raphinha's arrival at Elland Road caught the vast majority of Leeds' supporters on the hop. He was an unknown name signed from an obscure club –Rennes in France. The fee, £17 million, was unremarkable by Premiership standards during a close season which had seen Leeds spend two and a half times that amount in the acquisition of Rodrigo and Diego Llorente from Spanish clubs. But little did the fans know that Marcelo Bielsa had been closely following the 23-year-old Brazilian's progress for several years while he was playing first in Portuguese football then in French.

His full moniker, Raphael Dias Belloli, revealed his partly Italian heritage through his father and he has Italian nationality in addition to Brazilian. Without any English, it wasn't surprising that at Leeds he gravitated towards Rodrigo, whose first language is Portuguese and who indeed was born in Brazil, not arriving in Spain until he was in his early teens.

In his first interview-with his translated answers voiced-over by a guy with a broad Yorkshire accent, much to the amusement of fans –Raphinha said he'd been watching the Premiership on TV since he was a boy in Restinga, a suburb of Porto Alegre. He liked what he saw and it was always his ambition to play in the Prem because "it's where all the best players are." But Leeds United particularly appealed to him because he was "enchanted by their style." So far from being daunted by working with a demanding manager such as Marcelo Bielsa, he welcomed the prospect claiming that was exactly what he needed to get the best out of him. His only regret was that, in the present circumstances, fans weren't allowed in stadiums, which was robbing football of its magic. As for himself, he liked to express himself on the pitch, even have fun and bring joy to the spectators. At the same time he would perform with maximum dedication. All things considered, Raphinha, a gaunt, artistic looking guy, seemed the incarnation of the old school Brazilian footballer, the type all football followers still identify with Brazil despite the years of dismal Dungas and fractious geezers like David Luiz.

Marcelo Bielsa decided to carefully nurture Raphinha, bringing him on as a late sub and thus giving him time to adjust to the hurly-burly of the Premiership. First seen at Villa Park, he raced on the pitch in his tracksuit to joyfully acclaim Patrick Bamford's opening goal. Bielsa quickly made clear to him that concentration must be maintained and restraint exercised at all times. When he finally pulled on the shirt after Bamford's hat-trick had sealed victory, he moved with a raking quarter-miler's stride and rolled a pass which stopped as dead as a crown green bowls wood. It was moved on to Hernandez who, however, slipped as he was shooting.

Coming on as a sub at Selhurst Park, he continued to impress with his dedicated tracking back and even more so with a 30 yard free kick, delivered in classic Brazilian style which grazed a Crystal Palace post before it went out.

His full debut was at home to Arsenal when he showed his strength on the ball by brushing aside Willian's tackle as if it was a midget's challenge. Shooting from 25 yards, his strike flew a foot wide and, vexed with his own inaccuracy, he frowned and shouted "no-oh!"

In a game which Leeds fully deserved to win and in which both Bamford and Rodrigo had struck the frame of the goal, Raphinha was similarly foiled when, receiving a pass when off-balance, he contrived to lash a shot which rebounded high from a Gunners' post.

Seemingly downhearted by his narrow failure to get on the scoresheet, he was reassured by Kalvin Phillips who told him "you're bound to, mate, it's only a matter of time!" In the very next game his teammate's prophecy was borne out when he scored at Goodison Park with a low dipping shot which left Pickford helpless.

By now Raphinha was fully integrated into the side. It was blatantly obvious that he was head and shoulders above Helder Costa in skill and especially in attitude.

Raphinha was happy as Larry when Rodrigo suggested they give the others a taste of Brazilian music in the dressing room. It went down well with Jack Harrison in particular acclaiming the pair of them as "really happy, friendly guys", and saying samba rhythms were right up his street.

When Leeds went to Old Trafford, some pundits snickered when Raphinha was caught napping by the rugged Luke Shaw in the opening minute triggering the move which led to United's first goal. Switched to the other wing by Bielsa, he soon cut Wan-Bissaka down to size. Sadly Raphinha would be robbed of a wonder goal only by an incredible point-blank save from David de Gea. Receiving an excellent cross from Rodrigo, he needed no time to trap it, firing a ferocious volley which, after the United keeper had somehow kept it out, saw the ball flying upwards in a weird parabola glancing first off the bar and then off the far post before Maguire's desperate clearance.

With commentators gleefully extolling United's 6-2 victory, few pointed out that had Raphinha scored with this extraordinary effort, the deficit at that moment would have stood at four-two, a far more accurate reflection of the gap between the two sides.

At the Hawthorns against West Bromwich, Stuart Dallas, playing a blinder, saw Raphinha wide to his right and promptly found him. Raphinha cut in full of menace eager to join in the goal spree. With a lateral run across the edge of the box he jinked between Peltier and Ivanovic before fiercely flashing an absolute sabre blade of a shot beyond the full stretch Johnstone and depositing it perfectly high in the top corner.

Raphinha opened the scoring away at Newcastle receiving a perfect pass from Rodrigo and steering the ball immaculately home with a first-time shot through a crowded goalmouth.

Later, sensing that Patrick Bamford was completely off his game, Raphinha totally ignored him, not passing when Bamford seemed well placed to score. Just before that Rodrigo's shot had been blocked only for him to smartly backheel the rebound to Raphinha sprinting full tilt into an overlap. Raphinha took the ball in his stride, nipped past a defender and moved right to the dead ball line whence he shot hard beyond keeper Darlow who was staggered to see the ball cannoning off the near post. This was an extraordinary incident –was there any justification for Raphinha to ignore Bamford or was it just sheer greed on his part to score from an 'impossible' angle?

Bamford decided to have a friendly word with Raphinha after the match but, given that the Brazilian speaks little English, he did so in French. Raphinha, who thus far could only converse in Portuguese with Rodrigo and Helder Costa, was pleasantly surprised and thenceforth a bond was established based on a shared second language.

Newcastle were fighting back fiercely and, in the determination to keep the Geordies out, Ayling and Raphinha collided leaving the Brazilian lying flat on his back. He recovered but was soon knocked down again by a foul from Fabian Schar. With a cheerful 'let's get on with it' gesture Ayling told him "at least it wasn't me this time!" Raphinha had seemed puzzled by English humour when he first joined Leeds but a belated smile showed he was getting the hang of it now.

Though Newcastle equalised with a finely worked goal, it was only four minutes before Leeds regained the lead with a superb seven man, eight pass goal. Raphinha was at the heart of it with an exquisite high pass to Jack Harrison. Half dinked, half floated, it bamboozled the Geordies' defence before Harrison showed consummate skill to curl the ball round the diving Darlow.

After Newcastle's dangerous dribbler, St Maximin came on as a sub, the very next minute Raphinha, so far in splendid form with one goal and one assist to his name, unaccountably decided to perpetrate a long high back pass which unsurprisingly took Meslier clean off guard and led to a totally unnecessary corner.

Marcelo Bielsa was utterly appalled, stepping beyond his technical zone and bellowing a rebuke to Raphinha-he must never attempt such arrogant nonsense again. It was fortunate for the Brazilian that his moment of madness didn't result in a goal but it very nearly did. From Shelvey's corner, Newcastle centre back Jamaal Lascelles, challenged in the air by both Roberts and Cooper, narrowly managed to get a head on the ball which struck the top of the bar before slithering to safety along the roof of the net. Even then there was Mr Taylor's judgement to cope with and he deemed that Lascelles' header actually struck Cooper and thus a second corner was awarded. Fortunately Luke Ayling booted it clear.

Having learned his lesson, Raphina was majestic in the King Power Stadium against Leicester. In a wonderful seven-man, nine-pass move which narrowly failed to produce an early opener, he was the key figure in a tremendous transition, picking up Rodrigo's thirty yard pass before delivering a sublime flighted cross straight to Bamford.

After sustaining a knock in the closing stages at Leicester, Raphinha recovered quickly to face Everton at Elland Road. Though he was at fault for Everton's first goal with an irresolute challenge which led Lucas Digne to deliver a telling cross, he pulled one back for the Whites early in the second half. Receiving the ball in a goalmouth skirmish, he promptly passed it into the net. This was the extraordinary thing about Raphinha, his ability to strike for goal without even the merest preliminary touch let alone a trap!

He lit up the home game against Crystal Palace with an astounding piece of trickery which saw him combine a drag back with a backheel nutmeg of Gary Cahill leaving the bemused defender to frantically throw him down only centimetres outside the box. No goal resulted from the free kick but later it was Raphinha's fierce shot -which Guaita could only desperately parry- from which Bamford doubled Leeds' lead. Had Cahill not fouled him in the earlier incident, it's conceivable that Raphinha would have gone one to score a sublime individual goal in the manner of Eddie Gray, the Peacocks' legendary master of dragback, swerve and shimmy, the great Glaswegian who made Leeds fans laugh out loud with delight as he fooled defences with his outrageous skill.

By now the media had belatedly wised up to Raphinha's superb individual ability and were unpleasantly speculating about his sale value at the end of the season. Meanwhile, Marcelo Bielsa, calmly responding to questions about the young Brazilian winger, merely observed that he did some things well and other things not so well. Bielsa clearly recognised the need to keep media praise from going to Raphinha's head.

Raphinha continued to shine. Against Crystal Palace his fierce parried shot helped Bamford to score. Then against Wolves, in the continuing absence of both Rodrigo and Phillips, he assumed responsibility for free kicks. His perfectly floated deliveries would certainly have resulted in goals had it not been for a world class goalkeeping display by Ruy Patricio. Raphinha himself was foiled by the Portuguese custodian in the final minute of the match when he somehow clawed aside the Brazilian's powerful header just as it was about to go in at the near post.

Against Southampton Raphinha was foiled of a goal after spearheading Stuart Dallases' devastating counter only by Romeu's phenomenal tackle just as he was in the act of scoring. On other occasions the Brazilian set up teammates with perfect passes and cutbacks only to see them waste the chances he provided. The culprits included Roberts, who first blasted the ball over the bar and later shot yards wide, Llorente, who needed more power in his close range strike, and Costa who ballooned the ball into the stand.

In the final stages of the match Raphinha scored himself with an immaculate freekick to which McCarthy had no answer. Raphinha then fell victim to an avoidable booking when he removed his shirt to display a message in Portuguese commemorating the life of the recently deceased mother of Brazilian superstar Ronaldinho. If Raphinha had mentioned his praiseworthy plan to his teammates beforehand he could have followed Stuart Dallases' example in displaying a replica shirt to avoid the referee's sanction.

Not that this made any difference to Sky co-commentator Andy Hinchcliffe who was rhapsodizing about Raphinha for the entire match, ignoring significant contributions by other Leeds' players. It was one thing to acknowledge the Brazilian's superb technical skill -it was another to indulge in foolish 'Raphinha Mania.'

As a matter of fact, Raphinha came down to earth in the very next match, at home to Aston Villa. He was far below his best, let down frequently by his first touch. What's more, he should have equalised in the closing minutes when he mistimed his header from a sumptuous Harrison cross. He looked the picture of misery at the final whistle, slumped in front of the ad boards, downcast at having-just for once-let his teammates down.

Raphinha was still somewhat below his best away to West Ham but he was back on song at home to Chelsea when he instigated a lightning counter with a great ball curled into Bamford's path. Sadly Bamford was flagged marginally offside as he squared the ball for Tyler Roberts' tap in.

Then Raphinha was denied what looked like a certain goal by a phenomenal save from his ex-Rennes' teammate, keeper Edouard Mendy. Receiving Rodrigo's knockdown with his back to goal, the Brazilian brilliantly swivelled on the penalty spot and fired for the bottom left corner. Mendy had dived the opposite way but, readjusting at the last split second, he was sitting down as he somehow palmed the ball to safety with his left glove.

Against Fulham at Craven Cottage, Raphinha was subjected to rough treatment which had the entire Leeds' bench raising their voices in vehement protest.The worst incident came when he was brutally sandwiched between Anguissa and Ola Aina and sent crashing down. As Pablo Quiroga flashed five fingers at referee Coote to indicate the Camerounian's foul total, Mr Coote naively indicated accidental infringements. In actual fact Anguissa's kick on the heel and Ola Aina's simultaneous ankle stamp recalled the treatment meted out to Pele, Raphinha's illustrious predecessor at the World Cup in England in 66.

Fortunately Raphinha soon recovered and had the last laugh when he nonchalantly trapped Bamford's pass, shrugged off Tete and prodded the winning goal. The Brazilian winger's effortless agility and balance was revealed yet again.

Raphinha had yet to make his way into the Leeds side when the Whites played Manchester City at Elland Road. But, six months later, his reputation had clearly preceded his appearance at the Etihad. He wasn't at his best that day, so out of sorts with his corner kicking that Phillips had to deputise. That said, Raphinha was working harder than the Sky Blues had probably anticipated. When he dispossessed Sterling with a perfectly executed sliding tackle, he ended up with his forearm trodden on by the England international-and no sanction incurred.

Posted as a potentially dangerous outball when Leeds were reduced to ten men, it looked odds-on that Raphinha would score the winner when he found himself one-on-one with Ederson after Kalvin Phillips' splendid 30 yard pass. Yet he had to acknowledge with a wry grin the impeccable tackle whereby his compatriot foiled him.

It was a totally different story at the very end when he trapped Fernandinho's misplaced pass and burst forward. He was subjected to a violent bodycheck by the disgruntled City captain making no attempt to go for the ball as he raced back after Raphinha. Yet Andre Marriner took no action about an infringement which was far worse than the one for which he'd dismissed Liam Cooper. Indeed it resulted in Raphinha sustaining a haematoma and missing three matches as a result.

At last Raphinha was looking like his old self again when Leeds faced Southampton away. First he tormented the Malian Djenepo with foot on ball trickery combined with a nutmeg. But as he looked to dribble on the dead ball line, Djenepo hooked his legs from under him. It should of course have been a free kick yet Peter Bankes awarded a corner, from which nothing came.

Early in the second half Raphinha was at the heart of a stunning Leeds' move which deserved a goal. Free on the right touchline, his instant lob seemed nonchalant yet, when Rodrigo chested the ball down to Dallas, the Ulsterman leaned into a thunderous half volley cross shot which was hurtling towards just inside the far post only for Alex McCarthy to bring off a wonderful save.

Later it was the Brazilian who sized up danger at one forward glance and delivered a fine curling ball beyond Vestergaard bouncing into Bamford's path. It would almost certainly have produced a goal if referee Peter Bankes had awarded a penalty when McCarthy tried to trip Leeds' centre forward.

Without doubt Raphinha was back to his brilliant best and, fed with a fine crossfield ball from Struijk, he surged into a marvellous dribble going effortlessly past Salisu and Walker- Peters then dodging beyond Stephens, moving along the edge of the box before shooting powerfully only for his shot to fly over over the bar.

Leeds' revelation of a right-winger showed he had a sense of humour when he received a cutback from Bamford and steered the ball effortlessly into the net. He doubtless anticipated that Bamford would be given offside. Hearing the roars of relief from the crowd when that happened, he laughed before humorously pulling his shirt halfway up in pseudo- celebration.

The final match of the season, against West Bromwich on May 23, gave the newly re-admitted spectators –8000 of them–the opportunity not only to salute old heroes but to acclaim new ones. Foremost among the latter was the Brazilian revelation Raphael Dias Belloli, known by his footballing name Raphinha. The object of fascinated scrutiny by fans in the Norman Hunter End when he strode over to the corner flag in the 17th minute, he obliged with a perfect delivery which cleared Gaetano Berardi's leap and bounced up dangerously in the goalmouth where it was attacked by Jack Harrison and Rodrigo with the Spaniard being the one to head the ball home. The fans behind the goal were celebrating face-to-face with half a dozen White shirts. The ones by the flag yelled for Raphinha to join his teammates. Smiling from ear to ear he duly did so. This was what the Brazilian really loved, interaction with passionate fans delighting in his skill.

Whilst supporters who'd been glued to the TV throughout the season knew that Raphinha could be relied on to work hard in defence, it was another thing to see him in the flesh tackling back and preventing the Chelsea loanee Gallagher from exploiting Alioski's misplaced pass. Later Raphinha was on the receiving end of a vengeful tackle by Gallagher who was the target of booing from then on.

Another aspect of Raphinha's manifold skills was the ability to effortlessly swing dangerous aerial balls from deep positions. One of these might well have led to a goal for either Rodrigo or Harrison had it not been for referee David Coote's punctilious action in whistling for Rodrigo's sturdy challenge on Kyle Bartley.

While Raphinha's powerful shooting was not in evidence this time, he had laid on excellent passes for Hernandez and Bamford. Even as Leeds' supporters were singing the praises of the departing Pablo, they consoled themselves in the knowledge that another great Latin artist had arrived at Elland Road.

ALWAYS A WORKER, SOMETIMES MORE THAN THAT

TYLER ROBERTS

Tyler Roberts arrived at Elland Road while still in his teens, signed from West Bromwich Albion six months before Marcelo Bielsa became head coach. Bielsa was quick to note the lad's versatility –he could play as an attacking midfielder, as an outright winger or as a striker. Yet, considered purely as a striker, his 1:7 goals to games ratio would clearly not be sufficient to make him a regular first teamer. On the other hand, Roberts, though born in Gloucester of mixed Jamaican and Welsh heritage, had opted to represent Wales and thus would benefit from international experience.

At the beginning of the Premiership season, Bielsa gave Roberts a chance, bringing him on at Anfield as a substitute after Patrick Bamford, already a goalscorer, faded slightly in the second half. Roberts could make no impression and, when Bamford soon established himself as a regular goalscorer, the Welshman was confined to the bench.

The other possibility for Roberts was as an attacking midfielder and, whilst his finishing remained weak, he was a good passer of the ball. When Rodrigo was fit and well, his level of skill was far beyond that of Tyler Roberts but the Spaniard's illness and subsequent groin injury opened the door.

Reappearing as a sub, in place of Klich, against Everton, Roberts worked tirelessly as always but missed a great chance to score when the Toffees left him unmarked just inside the area and Bamford found him with an excellent pass straight to his boot. With all the time in the world to shoot and only the keeper to beat, Tyler walloped the ball high over the bar, covering his face in mortification.

Tyler Roberts' real breakthrough came on February 14 at the Emirates. Although Leeds were badly beaten 4-2 that day, three of the goals they conceded had come in the first half before Roberts came on in place of Klich. Closely instructed and encouraged from the touchline by Marcelo Bielsa, he worked tirelessly in defence and was a constant threat to Arsenal in attack.

In the 68th minute Roberts nimbly evaded Bellerin and delivered a perfect cutback for fellow substitute Helder Costa who swerved past Xaka and scored, thus halving the deficit after Struijk had registered with a header.

Tyler's skill on the ball was notable when he played a full part in a wonderful bout of first time passing alongside Raphinha and Bamford which should have led to a penalty after Bamford was brought down. Then, in stoppage time Roberts sent Jamie Shackleton clean through with a splendid pass only to see Shackleton misfire with a volley.

Roberts deservedly kept his place against Wolves and Marcelo Bielsa was pleased to observe his unrelenting work rate. This was an aspect of the Welshman's game which rightly commended itself to the fans even as they chuckled at Tyler's shout of anguish when, dashing up at full speed, he narrowly failed to get on the end of a

Raphinha shot angled across the goalmouth just before it went out of play.

Late in the game Roberts was wrongly deprived of his first assist. Trapping Pablo Hernandez' fine through ball, he excelled with a perfectly weighted pass for Bamford. Bamford exploded a devastating strike beyond the keeper only to have it scrubbed off at Stockley Park by a hair's breadth.

Against Southampton Tyler Roberts again turned provider for Patrick Bamford with an excellent ball from which Bamford outwitted the two Saints' centre backs and scored. Marksmanship, however, remained his besetting weakness. Prompted by Raphinha, he wasted a more than decent early chance by blasting the ball over the bar. Early in the second half he should have profited from a perfect Raphinha cutback. Standing unmarked, he shot yards wide and covered his face in dismay.

Leeds' home game against Aston Villa produced a match in which rookie referee Peter Bankes was far too tolerant of borderline challenges from the Midlanders. Roberts allowed himself to be provoked by the sheer nastiness of fullback Matt Targett and, after threatening to hurl the ball at the offender, he was promptly booked.

Tyler Roberts' run of games as a regular seemed to come to an end when he trudged off resignedly at the London Stadium in the latter stages of the game against West Ham. But, although Rodrigo reappeared after six matches absent injured, he was a sad shadow of his former self.

Brought back into the fold for the home game against Chelsea, Tyler Roberts was unlucky not to find himself on the scoresheet. At first this would have been a simple tap in when he was unmarked and the narrowly offside Bamford squared the ball to him. But, with fifteen minutes gone, after neat interpassing with Bamford, Tyler turned suddenly and delivered a wonderful swirling lob which seemed bound for the net. Yet Chelsea's excellent Senegalese keeper Edouard Mendy brought off a superb save leaping high and using his fingertips to touch the ball against the bar whence it rebounded for Rudiger to blast clear.

Roberts had a mixed game against Fulham at Craven Cottage. He prevailed on Patrick Bamford's unselfishness when he called for a ball to be left to him despite the fact that Bamford was already embarrassing the crude Danish defender Joachim Anderson who was on the edge of the area and desperately holding Leeds' centre forward. Bamford did as he was asked but, before Roberts could profit from that, Tosin had dashed in to boot the ball away.

Later Roberts was harshly deprived of an assist after Luke Ayling had leaped onto his fine hanging cross to loop a header over the keeper. When Fulham prevailed on the referee to consult Stockley Park, they cancelled it on the grounds of Roberts being offside. Yet the margin shown on the TV picture was ridiculously narrow.

Against Sheffield United Tyler was fortunate not to sustain serious injury when he was violently tackled and sent hurtling through the air by George Baldock. Baldock ought to have been sent off but escaped doubtless because he was being checked for concussion.

Tyler Roberts, who figured only as a substitute at Anfield, now started against Liverpool in the reverse fixture. Working hard as always, he showed intermittent glimpses of skill but, once again, his finishing was feeble. After a good cutback from Harrison he could only shoot straight at the keeper. An even better opportunity presented itself in the closing stages when Leeds were pressing hard for a deserved equaliser. Picking up a good square pass from Poveda, Roberts evaded the floundering Kabak yet with Alisson completely at his mercy, he contrived to smack the ball straight at the keeper's chest.

Coming on as a late substitute against Southampton, Tyler Roberts scored in stoppage time when goalkeeper McCarthy parried Bamford's shot straight to him. Roberts kept his cool and steered the ball home. He was beside himself with delight finally scoring a Premiership goal. Luke Ayling and Stuart Dallas were made up for him and lifted him from his jubilant knee slide while the entire Leeds' bench erupted with joy at victory being clinched thanks to an unexpected scorer.

ILLNESS, INJURY-AND GLIMPSES
OF GREAT SKILL

RODRIGO

When Marcelo Bielsa signed Rodrigo from cash-strapped Valencia on August 29 2020, it seemed like a wise move. The fee, admittedly a record for Leeds United, was modest by European standards at 30 million euro. And Rodrigo was a Spanish international who'd figured at the 2018 World Cup.

He was noted for skill and intelligence –hardly surprising in that his Brazilian father Adalberto had relocated to Vigo in Spain specifically to start a football school. Born in Rio, Rodrigo Moreno Machado was in his early teens when he accompanied his parents to Spain. Adalberto's business partner was the Brazilian international full-back Mazinho and Rodrigo soon became close friends with Mazinho's two sons, Thiago Alcantara (who went on to fame with Barcelona and Bayern Munich) and Rafina. The boys soon learnt Spanish and acquired Spanish nationality.

As a lad of 18, Rodrigo was playing for Real Madrid's B team. Picked out as a brilliant prospect by Manuel Pellegrini, he was brusquely discarded by Jose Mourinho who preferred strikers built like tanks. Transferred to Benfica, Rodrigo was promptly loaned for a year to Bolton Wanderers. Though he failed to set the Championship on fire, he soon picked up solid conversational English.

After returning to Benfica, Rodrigo was transferred to Valencia for €30 million and it was at the Mestalla that he made his name. His 1 to 3.5 goals per game ratio established him as a striker but not only did he better that with Spain but he contributed numerous assists for club and country. In addition he was widely respected as a dedicated footballer who never sought media limelight, an unassuming guy devoted to his beautiful partner Mari Martinez and their young daughter.

Rodrigo made his Leeds debut, a fortnight after signing, in a game against Liverpool at Anfield. It proved disastrous. Brought on as a substitute for the tiring Bamford around the hour mark, he contributed little and, with only three minutes left of normal time, his clumsy challenge on Fabinho conceded a penalty which Salah duly converted. This deprived Leeds of what would otherwise have been a fully merited 3-3 draw.

Carefully shielded by Bielsa after his blunder, Rodrigo reappeared against Manchester City as a second-half substitute after a two-game absence. His impact was immediate. Swerving away from Dias, he lambasted a shot which left the City crossbar shaking. Amazingly City's excellent keeper, Ederson was ruled to have got a fingertip to it. But, in an irony typical of football, Ederson made a total mess of the corner pawing at it pathetically and leaving Rodrigo, whose brilliant strike had been denied, with a simple tap in.

At Villa Park it was Patrick Bamford's sublime hat-trick which caught the headlines. But it was Rodrigo who orchestrated Leeds' wonderful display. In particular, he prompted Bamford's opening goal. He cleverly picked out Harrison then raced to the box, full of menace. When Harrison returned the compliment, the rugged Glaswegian McGinn desperately tried to dispossess him.

But McGinn ended up flat on his back as the Spaniard checked his stride before firing in a fierce angled shot which Argentinian keeper Martinez could only parry leaving Bamford to ram the ball home from close range.

When it came to Bamford's third goal, once again it was Rodrigo who laid the foundation with a wonderful 35 yard pass hit with underspin to Costa, after which the Portuguese winger linked with Shackleton to find Bamford.

Rodrigo's display against Villa had been so outstanding that even the element among the fans who craved Pablo Hernandez' return were mollified. What's more, Marcelo Bielsa's faith in a player of high skill with an acute football brain had been vindicated.

Then fate intervened. Rodrigo was stricken with Covid. Obliged to sit out two 4-1 defeats – against Leicester City and Crystal Palace – Rodrigo returned with 17 minutes left of the home game with Arsenal. Despite the Gunners being down to 10 men after Pepe was sent off, the match seemed bound to end in a goalless draw. Indeed it did yet Rodrigo transformed Leeds in those closing stages.

Moving in from the right to shoot left-footed in his preferred manner, Rodrigo's fierce curled drive looked goalbound but missed by a fraction. With 11 minutes left, Leeds were narrowly baulked of what would have been a great goal. Koch advanced through the centre circle, Rodrigo gestured for a pass and Koch neatly found him with a 15 yard ball inside the defender. Rodrigo, on the edge of the box, surged past Xaka and Gabriel and fired off a shot. Keeper Leno could get nowhere near it and it cannoned high off the angle of post and bar before drifting out of play. Rodrigo didn't expostulate, merely framed his face within his hands, very calm and self-possessed.

Rodrigo was beginning to strike up a strong understanding with Raphinha and, when the Brazilian struck the post in the closing seconds, it had been Rodrigo's glancing header which had found him.

Sadly the effects of Long Covid started to tell on Rodrigo. He was used mostly as a substitute and, even when he resumed against West Ham on December 11 in what was-almost incredibly- only his fourth start of the season, he looked nothing like his earlier self.

Marcelo Bielsa varied his deployment of Rodrigo against Newcastle, deciding to let him start the game and seeing how long he might last before tiredness overcame him. It worked a treat. Moving cleverly between the two big centre backs, Rodrigo noted that keeper Darlow had come out too far and looped a header over him which rebounded from the bar to let Bamford equalise.

Then Rodrigo scored with a great diving header from 10 yards out to give Leeds the lead. It followed superb combination play with Jack Harrison beginning when Rodrigo picked out the winger with a fine left foot cross and Harrison returned the compliment with an even better one.

When Rodrigo began to feel the effects of his efforts, he went off to be replaced by Pablo Hernandez who, coming on with fresh legs, contributed two assists in as many minutes. Bielsa had shown great astuteness in his deployment of two highly skilful players.

After what happened at Old Trafford, pundits pounced on Rodrigo's misplaced pass which found Dan James and led to one of United's goals. They largely ignored the fact that Bamford should have equalised in the opening minutes but failed to do so despite the lovely glided pass from Rodrigo which set him up.

By this stage of the season Rodrigo and Raphina had established an excellent rapport and it was Rodrigo's wonderful floated cross to his Brazilian buddy which enabled Raphina to hammer the ferocious first-time shot which was only kept out by a phenomenal world-class save by de Gea.

In what was a very difficult match Rodrigo had tried desperately hard to stem United's flow but had been let down by his midfield partner Klich whose workrate left a lot to be desired.

West Bromwich were of course a far easier proposition and Leeds swept them aside five nil with Rodrigo starting and finishing a fine move involving Phillips, Dallas and Klich. From deep in his own half he set off on a high stepping run which concluded with him scoring via a deflection.

Against Newcastle in the return fixture at St James Park, he showed all his skill, intelligence and not least his blossoming partnership with Raphina when he waited for the Brazilian to complete his overlap and then deftly back heeled a pass straight into his path resulting in Raphina striking a post.

Before that the pair of them had done even better when Rodrigo nonchalantly accepted a fine pass from Bamford, turned and looked round surveying his options. He passed perfectly to Raphina who scored with a first-time shot.

Later Rodrigo sent a 30 yard pass bouncing perfectly into Raphina's stride path and Stuart Dallas narrowly failed to convert the winger's pass with a diving header.

When Leeds cancelled Newcastle's equaliser after only four minutes, the plaudits went quite rightly to Jack Harrison and Raphina. Even so it was Rodrigo who instigated the move by prompting Raphina.

It was surely no coincidence that Rodrigo's best performances had coincided with Leeds' finest team displays. True, their best so far came at the King Power Stadium when the Spanish playmaker injured his groin stretching for a misplaced Alioski pass. What happened was that Mateusz Klich, sidelined by Bielsa after some lacklustre performances, stepped into the breach in the twentieth minute with a display combining brains and physical strength to bring down the highflying Leicester. Yet even before he was forced off, Rodrigo had been a key figure in a wondrous high speed transition which nearly led to a goal. Picking up a neat ball from Phillips, he'd sent Raphinha flying forward with a superb thirty yard pass to the right flank. Had Dallases' usually accurate radar not been marginally off kilter, Bamford would have surely completed the Peacocks' finest move of the season.

When Rodrigo eventually returned, it remained to be seen how well he and Klich could be jointly deployed to best effect. As things turned out, Klich had already been substituted by the time the Spaniard returned to the fray against West Ham on the hour mark after missing six matches. Inevitably rusty at first, he began to produce some elegant passes yet he should have been able to pull a goal back in the closing stages when Bamford jumped over a dangerous ball from Luke Ayling in the goalmouth. Bamford had counted on Rodrigo effortlessly finishing the job but the Spaniard found himself facing the never say die centre back scrapper Dawson, a bloke used to roughing it in the lower divisions. No sooner had Rodrigo squeezed his shot goalwards than Dawson was somehow scooping it off the goal line.

The long term effects of illness and injury kept Rodrigo on the sidelines for half a dozen games. Reappearing in May, Rodrigo didn't participate in the home game against Spurs until the 78th minute when he replaced Bamford. But the Spaniard got straightaway on his game, swapping fine passes with Harrison. Then he scored. Perfectly reading a four-man move from box to box, he combined coolness with power as he drilled his shot home.

Brought on by Marcelo Bielsa 11 minutes into the second half at Turf Moor to replace a Patrick Bamford buffeted by Burnley's belligerent defenders, within a minute of his introduction, Rodrigo's brilliant instant backheel freed Raphinha in the centre circle. As the move developed, Rodrigo sprinted into the box anticipating Harrison's cross from which he would have scored had Tarkowsky not got a last ditch boot on the ball to jab it out for a corner.

Then came Rodrigo's two absolute world-class goals. Moving into the D he benefited from a great pass from Harrison yet he killed the ball instantly with his left foot before swaying between

Ben Mee and Tarkowsky, hurdling Tarkowsky's extended leg then lobbing the ball over the bemused Peacock-Farrell flush into the back of the net.

A mere two minutes and seven seconds elapsed before an even finer fourth goal. Rodrigo ranged long-striding through the gaps in the Burnley defence and latched on to Harrison's wonderful pass beyond Taylor. With Tarkowsky trying in vain to thwart him and Peacock- Farrell rushing desperately out, Rodrigo demonstrated perfect balance as he swerved beyond Tarkowsky, pivoted and fired the ball over the keeper's fingertips into the back of the net. Leeds' substitutes captain Liam Cooper and Jamie Shackleton immediately showed their delight for a teammate long sidelined by injury to race out and hug him.

At the close of normal time Rodrigo looked as if he might even be in for a hat-trick when he instantly killed an Alioski cross but, challenged by Charlie Taylor, once of Leeds and now Burnley's best player, he shot just wide.

Rodrigo started from kick-off against Southampton in St Mary's Stadium. Though he took the first half to adjust to the role of supporting Patrick Bamford from an advanced midfield position, he hit full form early in the second half when he received a stabbed pass from Jack Harrison. What followed was sublime –Rodrigo wheeled beyond Ward-Prowse and took out two defenders with a fantastic reverse pass rolling to Bamford's feet just outside the six yard box. It took frantic defence from the Southampton rearguard to keep out a barrage of shots which followed.

Rodrigo rose to the same heights once again when he brought off a glorious chip taking out two midfielders and two defenders and delivering the ball first bounce to Bamford who scored.

Clearly in his element, Rodrigo seemed at times to have a quasi-telepathic understanding with Raphinha. What's more, he was clearly disgruntled when he was substituted only three minutes after assisting Bamford's goal. Leeds' bench were, however, concerned to conserve his energy after his recent long layoff.

Though the impact of Leeds' record signing Rodrigo had been diminished by the injuries he suffered during the season and by the effects of Long Covid, his brilliant outburst of goals against Spurs and Burnley signalled his full recovery. At Elland Road, on the final day, fans were eager to see him in action. There were roars of delight in the sixth minute when he dummied a clever Pablo Fernandez' chip enabling Jack Harrison to prod the ball home. Yet referee David Coote scrubbed the strike on the grounds that Rodrigo had distracted goalkeeper Sam Johnstone.

The fans didn't have long to wait. In the 17th minute Raphinha's splendidly flighted corner bounced up in the goalmouth and it was Rodrigo Moreno Machado who got in a stooping header to send the ball high into the back of the Baggies' net. Rodrigo's momentum took him on into the side netting and he briskly disentangled himself to punch the air with his fist right in front of a knot of delighted fans at the Norman Hunter End. One fan tried to reach him and was prevented by a steward but other supporters found themselves face-to-face with their heroes as Rodrigo's teammates hastened to hug him. Till then it had been the old stalwarts who'd been the objects of fan adoration but now a new hero was acclaimed- the jubilant scorer Rodrigo.

Rodrigo's combative and defiant attitude was just what the fans wanted to see and when he shook an angry fist after referee David Coote had belatedly pulled him up-for an alleged foul on Kyle Bartley after his header had sent Jack Harrison clear- they roared in support of him.

It was sad for Rodrigo that he wasn't selected for the Spanish Euros squad. Yet, more important, it afforded him the opportunity of a long Summer's rest to shake off any lingering effects of his illness before pulling on the White shirt again for the challenges which lie ahead.

LEEDS TO THE CORE

JAMIE SHACKLETON

There's no bigger fans' favourite at Elland Road than Jamie Shackleton. This isn't surprising. Born and bred in Leeds, he's said in interview "I've always given everything I've got every time I put the white shirt on" and "all I could ever ask for is to play for Leeds in the Premiership."

These comments stamp Shack as the quintessential LUFC lad, a product of the Academy who otherwise has little memorable to say in front of a camera. In some ways he's a bit old school, not fussed about hairstyles, not bothered with tattoos, a young bloke with a frank and open countenance. Early in his career there were opponents who thought they might face an easy task against someone only 5'6" tall. Once they were on the receiving end of a Shackleton tackle, they were rapidly disabused of that notion. Yet Jamie was also a student of the game, embarking on a course leading to a UEFA coaching licence when he was only 19 years old.

Coming on at Villa Park in Kalvin Philips' absence and with Struijk subbed off after only 22 minutes, Shackleton knew it was his big chance to shine in midfield and he was determined to take it. Within a couple of minutes he'd clipped a good pass to Stuart Dallas whose shot was only narrowly wide. Next he stopped Villa's vaunted Ollie Watkins in his tracks. It was a foul of course but BT pundit Robbie Savage's shout for a yellow card was well out of order.

The highlight of that game was of course Patrick Bamford's hat trick. But Jamie Shackleton played a part in the first goal and also in the third. For the opener he was running at full tilt when he scooped a neat pass to Rodrigo. Staggering from his momentum, he soon regained his balance dashing forward to act as a decoy. For the last he linked cleverly with Helder Costa to provide a pre-assist.

Rightly praised for his performance both on fansites and by shrewd observers such as Michael Brown, he kept his place against Leicester City. Sadly he struggled when he was deployed further forward. Giving it all he'd got, he picked up a slight knock and was substituted at half-time. After that, with Phillips returning from injury quicker than expected, Shackleton returned to the subs' bench.

It was once again in Philipses' absence that Shack next appeared, this time at the Emirates. Known for his versatility and willingness to play anywhere, he found himself deployed at right wing back. In the opening stages Leeds were struggling badly with Ayling off form, Struijk ill at ease in midfield and Meslier looking potentially disastrous. Yet Shackleton single-handedly rebuffed a dangerous Gunners' attack showing all his qualities-razor-sharp tackling, game intelligence and distributive skill. He shut down Arsenal's vaunted new boy Smith Rowe and left Ceballos flat on his backside before he looked to start a counter with a pass to Klich. Later he delivered a splendid 25 yard pass straight into Raphina's stride path.

Marcelo Bielsa's second-half redeployment switched Shackleton into midfield while Pascal Struijk dropped back. At once Leeds began to gel. Yet Shack's most brilliant moment came when he took part in a marvellous exchange of quickfire passing with Roberts and Raphina, the climax of which was his own delicate pass to Patrick Bamford which, had referee Stuart Atwell pointed to the spot after Bamford was barged down, would probably have reduced the deficit to 4-3.

Shack's never-say-die spirit was exemplified in stoppage time when he burst forward fastening onto a fine pass from Tyler Roberts and volleyed a shot on goal. Sadly he mistimed it but his boldness, reading of the game and will to win were there for all to see.

Jamie Shackleton retained his place, in Kalvin Phillips' continuing absence, against Wolves, playing in midfield from the start. He showed there were some things he could do better than Phillips such as taking part in quick close passing moves. But he couldn't begin to replicate Phillips' ability to stifle attacks and instigate dangerous counters.

THE INVISIBLE MAN

PASCAL STRUIJK

Arriving at Elland Road six months before Marcelo Bielsa, the 18-year-old Dutchman Pascal Struijk made little impression and even afterwards there was an element among the fans who took against him, feeling that he wasn't tough enough to play at centre back. But Bielsa thought different. Above all he knew that Struijk had been educated at Ajax and would have had the importance of good distribution from defence inculcated in him from an early age.

Struijk, burly, black haired and bearded, of partly Indonesian heritage on his father's side, looked like a cross between a musician and a weightlifter. Some fans were apprehensive when Bielsa brought him on against Barnsley but he vindicated his manager's faith with a solid display.

When Leeds arrived in the Premiership, Struijk was thrown in at the deep end at Anfield due to Cooper being injured on Scotland duty. He made up one half of a makeshift central defence with Robin Koch. But it was the German international who struggled rather than Struijk. Strictly speaking Struijk was at fault when his headed clearance from a Robertson free kick fell to Mo Salah. Yet the speed and ferocity of Salah's resulting goal was the mark of a truly world-class player. Against almost anybody else Struijk might have got away with it. And, in terms of distribution, he played a colossal long ball right into Harrison's path which, though nothing came of it, had Ajax stamped all over it.

As soon as Liam Cooper had recovered, Bielsa looked to establish a defensive partnership between him and Koch so Struijk returned to the subs' bench. When he came back it was at defensive midfield as a replacement for the injured Kalvin Phillips at Villa Park. The position didn't seem to suit him, he looked edgy and was booked early on for a trip which sent Jack Grealish sprawling. When he committed another foul shortly afterwards, Bielsa removed him rather than risking a red card.

It was only after the Chelsea game which saw Koch receive a serious injury and Diego Llorente unable to complete 90 minutes that Struijk returned to the fold. He was one of several players who struggled at Old Trafford when his shin-clipping challenge on Martial brought a penalty which Fernandes converted.

Yet from around the turn of the year Pascal Struijk began to establish himself as a solid defender, one who wasn't injury prone, comfortable on the ball and confidently inter-passing with Liam Cooper in a style more relaxed than Leeds had previously shown. Whereas in the first eight games in the Premiership, the team had conceded 17 goals, in the next 8 they only let in 8.

The only fault that any reasonable observer could find with Pascal was his inability to score himself. He was in fine form against Leicester and was poised to net from close range when Ricardo Pereira foiled him in a last split second block with his boot studs.

Before that Struijk had played a key part when the Whites took the lead. Seizing on an error by Pereira, he brushed the whining Perez aside and promptly found Raphinha who assisted Bamford's goal. As well as that, Struijk initiated the counter-attack which led to Harrison's goal. His bold diving defensive header not only rebuffed Leicester but at the same time set up Dallas to drive forward.

While his teammates were fully appreciative of Struijk's contribution-not least Kalvin Phillips, who jocularly dubbed the towering Dutchman 'Young Pascal', the media scarcely noticed it. They went overboard, rightly so, about Bamford's devastating goal and Raphina's sublime skill but for them Pascal Struijk was the invisible man. Their routine references mispronounced his name as either 'Stroyk' or 'Strowk' and once even 'Strewick'(whereas in actual fact the nearest English equivalent to the daunting Dutch dipthong would be 'Strike') and his so-called 'air kick' was scoffed at till cameras revealed he'd been thwarted of a goal by Pereira's boot studs. As for his part in two goals, these received not a mention.

While scribes faltered over the spelling of his surname, Marcelo Bielsa, wary after his battle with the name 'Ipswich', of all northern European pronunciations, always referred to his central defender simply as 'Pascal.'

In contrast to Englishmen's difficulties with the pronunciation of his surname, Pascal Struijk's English, which he learnt in Amsterdam from the age of four onwards, was almost faultless and some fans reckoned he was picking up a trace of Yorkshire accent. If he hesitated in interview it was only because he wished to make an intelligent point. He showed himself capable of self scrutiny when he remarked that he needed to copy the English players' loud talking.

The media's invisible man did not escape the focus of Belgium's astute Spanish manager Roberto Martinez. Martinez was well aware that Struijk had been born in Belgium and was thus eligible for the national side. He hoped to sign him up before the Netherlands could claim him. Either way you looked at it was a plus for Leeds United.

Whoever he represented, it was vital for Struijk to play as a central defender not in midfield.

His unease in the latter role showed when Marcelo Bielsa, in a very rare strategic error, deployed him there in Phillips' absence against Arsenal at the Emirates.

After Bielsa had a rethink at half time, Struijk resumed his blossoming central defensive partnership with Liam Cooper. Sadly by then Leeds were three nil down. Although the final scoreline was 4-2, Struijk had the satisfaction of registering his first goal for the club. It was a perfectly timed titanic header from a corner where he outjumped the Gunners' centre back David Luiz and the ball fairly thundered off his napper into the back of the net.

Away against Wolves, Struijk was defensively solid and he was unlucky not to score when the shot he hooked round Dendoncker, reared up as it flew towards Ruy Patricio. Unfortunately the Portuguese keeper, though unsighted by Saiss, brought off an incredible parry. Struijk seized on it and lashed a second shot goalwards. A defender got in a block, the ball looped upwards and Struijk went down as if poleaxed after a nasty clash of heads. He lay prone till the attack petered out then got to his feet none the worse for wear.

At home against the hitherto prolific Chelsea, Pascal Struijk formed a central defensive partnership with Diego Llorente which looked the Whites' best combination so far. Whilst Diego Llorente caught the eye, Struijk was unobtrusively in all the right places at the right times.

Against Fulham, the Nigerian striker Josh Maja never got clear of Struijk and, when Parker opted for Serbian muscle at half time, Aleksander Mitrovic got no change out of him.

After Liam Cooper was sent off shortly before half-time at the Etihad, it was Pascal Struik who took his place. Some Leeds' fans were surprised that Marcelo Bielsa preferred him to Robin Koch. True, Koch, who came on instead of Roberts with half an hour left, had relatively recently recovered from serious injury. Yet Koch, for all his intelligent reading of the game, lacked the physical ruggedness of the burly Struijk. It was Struijk who played an important part alongside Diego Llorente at the heart of the defensive wall, rising time after time when City uncharacteristically resorted to crosses and decisively heading them well clear.

Pascal Struijk, an intelligent player who doubtless learned much from his baptism of fire against Liverpool at Anfield, proved a tower of strength in the reverse fixture. It was him who held the fort in the first half when Diego Llorente was below his best. Later the pair of them combined to confront the Reds with a stumbling block in central defence. Even so, Struijk got little credit from commentators. As far as Sky's Andy Hinchcliffe was concerned, Struijk received only the most perfunctory name mention for all his resolute play.

Pascal Struijk made an early impression in the home game against United, dispossessing McTominay with a sturdy tackle. His only error came a minute before half-time when he mistimed a tackle on Dan James and conceded a free kick albeit more than 25 yards out. This led to Meslier's wonderful save from Rashford.

In the second half Struijk's partnership with Llorente proved a bridge too far as far as United were concerned. The two centre backs perfectly complemented each other with the Spaniard's immaculate reading of the game and the Dutchman a colossus in the air, not to mention his sweeping long passes.

As he'd been schooled to do as a lad with Ajax, Struijk always looked beyond a solid defensive header to setting up a counterattack. It was just a pity that when he made a good clearance and simultaneously found Costa with a very fine pass, the Angolan could only lose control.

While Mason Greenwood had sporadically threatened Leeds in the first half, he ended the game as a blown fuse with Pascal Struijk simply too good for him.

For months Struijk had been an invisible man as far as the pundits were concerned but Ian Wright, more astute than his colleagues, broke the pattern on MOTD when he mentioned the Dutchman's name in the same breath as those of Kalvin Phillips and Diego Llorente as the men who'd done most to keep United at bay.

Against Tottenham Hotspur, Pascal Struijk and Diego Llorente faced their sternest task yet against Harry Kane and Son Yeung Min. Pissed off with himself after he failed to score an early goal when he volleyed over the bar from a corner, Struijk quickly shrugged it off. Neither he nor Llorente was to blame for Spurs' solitary goal but he was at his best in the second half when Bielsa switched him to marking Son-where his physical advantage against the lean and lanky South Korean would prove telling. First he hurled himself into a brilliant block when Son shot. Then came his stupendous tackle on the South Korean, combining rugged strength with impeccable timing and drawing roars of appreciation from the Whites' bench.

Having declined an opportunity to represent Belgium, the land of his birth, in Euro 2021, Pascal Struijk thanked head coach Roberto Martinez for his offer but stated that his "heart remained with the Netherlands." Regrettably he was excluded from the Dutch squad, an undeserved rebuff to a man who remained invisible to many who should have known better but was fully appreciated by Leeds' supporters for his stalwart defensive qualities.

PART THREE

LOOKING BACK ON 2020-1

Three games remained after Leeds defeated Spurs and in each of them the Whites swept aside mediocre opposition. To all intents and purposes, it was the crushing victory against Tottenham Hotspur which rang down the curtain on what had been a fabulously impressive season.

From first to last Leeds had played football as the game was meant to be played, in an all-out attacking style. Despite the misguided caveats of the pundits, this did not mean for a moment that Marcelo Bielsa's team was careless of defence, even less that the Peacocks' head coach prioritised style before substance. Only the sheer bad luck that both their centre back signings went down with serious injuries left them defensively vulnerable in the first half of the season.

Once the second half was underway the Leeds' rearguard was solid and, based on their performances in 2021, they would have finished fourth in the Premiership table. Lacking the financial means to compete with the likes of Manchester City, Manchester United, Liverpool and Chelsea, this was a fantastic achievement. And while Diego Llorente and Raphinha looked potentially world-class, the remaining regulars were Championship players each of whom took his game to another level after promotion had been achieved.

The three characteristics of Leeds United which endeared them to the huge audiences who delightedly followed them on TV were their teamwork, their team spirit and their sportsmanship. Their goals almost always followed superb build up play with long and short passes alternated, first-time touches varied with ambitious crossfield balls. And in an era when several of world football's most lauded stars –the likes of Ronaldo, Neymar and Pogba-were blatantly narcissistic, the modesty of Patrick Bamford, Stuart Dallas, Jack Harrison and Kalvin Phillips was totally refreshing. Furthermore, Leeds' sense of fair play, the very thing which had deservedly brought a FIFA award in 2019 –was undeniable.

There were elements among the Elland Road fanbase who'd been furious about Bielsa's decision to stand back and let Aston Villa score in that game. But in actual fact the decision was not only a noble one but something which imbued the Leeds' squad with a fully justified pride in their sportsmanship.

It was thus appropriate that Leeds played in an all-white strip, the very outfit which Don Revie had introduced decades earlier in honour of Real Madrid. That was of course not the Madrid of red card skulduggery Sergio Ramos but the alltime greats of yesteryear, artists such as Alfredo di Stefano and Ferenc Puskas.

A new generation of global admirers from Buenos Aires to Brisbane were irresistibly drawn to Leeds United because of their sparkling football. But in the city of Leeds itself Marcelo Bielsa was acclaimed with unmitigated fervour, murals painted in his image and streets renamed after him. A man of total modesty, he continued in his unpretentious lifestyle. Walking to work at Thorp Arch every day from his humble Wetherby abode, dressed in an LUFC tracksuit, he looked no different from a supporter from days long gone who'd stuck with the club through thick and thin.

There were those in the media who criticised Marcelo Bielsa for "not speaking English." Yet though he never mastered formal English, his command of everyday English was, as Kalvin Phillips put it, "surprisingly good." It was this that let him interact not only with the United squad but with the people he encountered in neighbourhood shops.

It was not long before Bielsa perceived a similarity between Leeds and his home city of Rosario in Argentina, a kinship which extended to the West Yorkshire countryside. But whereas in Rosario support's equally divided between Newell's Old Boys and Rosario Central, in Leeds there's a unique identification between the city and Leeds United. Bielsa knew this even before he was first appointed as head coach. It was what drew him to Leeds –plus the challenge of reviving the 'sleeping giant' of English football.

Throughout the long years of their exile from the Premiership – and even before –Leeds' supporters had felt a strong sense of grievance against their treatment by a media which fawned on metropolitan Chelsea and above all on the allegedly glamorous Manchester United. This surfaced in the interview conversations between Leeds' skipper Liam Cooper and dedicated Whites' fan, boxer and university graduate Josh Warrington when Cooper nodded as Warrington remarked –"you know what it means with Leeds – working class."

This sense of identity was well known to Leeds' owner Andrea Radrizzani and even more so to Director of Football Victor Orta. In April 2021 they immediately condemned the announcement of the proposed formation of a European Super League which had the backing of Liverpool, both Manchester clubs and Chelsea among others.

It was, however, Marcelo Bielsa whose criticism of the proposed ESL was the most trenchant. "Football belongs to everybody" he said "even if there are owners. The real owners of football are the ones who love the badge. Without them football would disappear. Any decision that affects all the people, all the fans of football and which privileges only one sector is staking the future."

With these words Bielsa gained the moral high ground for Leeds United whose supporters soon had the satisfaction of seeing the so-called European Super League utterly collapse and owners such as John W. Henry and Joel Glazer obliged to eat their words.

Printed in Great Britain
by Amazon